COPYCAT RECIPES

THE MOST POPULAR RECIPES FROM FAMOUS RESTAURANTS AROUND THE WORLD.

Sara Panera

TABLE OF CONTENTS

CHAPTER 8

OLD AND MODERN BREAD RECIPES

CHAPTER 9

SIDE SALAD RECIPES

CHAPTER 10

OLD AND MODERN SWEET AND SAVORY SNACK RECIPES

CHAPTER 11

OLD AND MODERN FRUIT SALAD RECIPES

INTRODUCTION

Thank you for purchasing our cookbook! The series of recipes selected by Sara Panera is having a great success, because Sara pays attention to every detail.

This cookbook brings together some of the most sought-after and appreciated recipes from around the world.

For each recipe our chefs have performed dozens and dozens of tests to make them as similar as possible to the original dish.

Always remember, though, that cooking is art and you can substitute the main ingredients with your favorite ingredients whenever you want!

Going to restaurants these days is difficult, which is why we're happy to help you bring the restaurant into your home!

You'll feel like you have your favorite chef sitting in your kitchen!

The secrets of famous dishes will be revealed to you and you can wow your whole family!

The recipes are organized by course so finding the dish that interests you will be easier.

What are you waiting for?

Choose your favorite food and start preparing it right away!

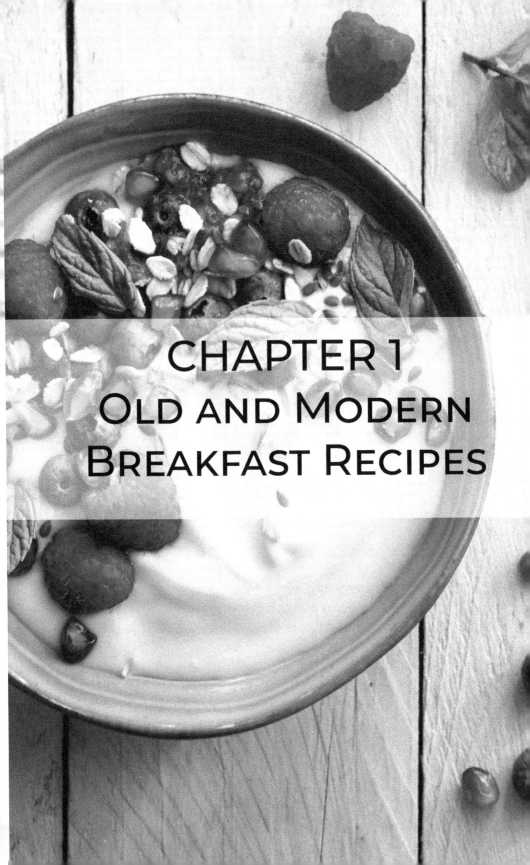

CHAPTER 1
Old and Modern Breakfast Recipes

1. Pillsbury Sweet Roll with Orange Juice

Preparation Time: 3 hours
Cooking Time: 30 minutes
Servings: 15

Ingredients:
Dough
- 2 1/4 teaspoons active dry yeast
- 1/2 cup warm water
- fresh orange zest; from 1 medium-sized orange
- 1/2 cup orange juice
- 1/4 cup sugar
- 1 teaspoon salt
- 1 large egg
- 2 Tablespoons unsalted butter; softened to room temperature
- 3 to 3.5 cups all-purpose flour

Filling
- 2 Tablespoons sugar
- 2 teaspoons ground cinnamon
- 1 Tablespoon unsalted butter; softened to room temperature

Glaze
- 1 cup confectioners' sugar
- 1 Tablespoon orange juice
- fresh orange zest; from 1 medium orange
- 1 teaspoon vanilla extract

Directions:
Make the Dough:
Dissolve the yeast in 1/2 cup warm water for about 1 minute. No need to use a thermometer for the water's temperature, but to be precise: about 105-115F degrees. Stir the yeast/water around. Then add orange zest, orange juice, sugar, salt, egg, butter, and 1.5 cups of flour. Beat everything together on low with a handheld mixer, scraping down the sides as needed.

(A mixer is definitely needed to break up all the butter and beat everything to the proper consistency.) With a wooden spoon, stir in enough of the remaining flour to make a dough easy to handle - about 1.5 - 2 more cups. You are looking for a dough that is not sticky and will spring back when poked with a finger.

Transfer the dough to a lightly floured surface and knead it with your hands for about 5-6 minutes. Form the dough into a ball and transfer it to a lightly greased bowl. Cover the dough and let sit in a warm place until doubled in size, about 1.5 hours.

Line the bottom of a 9x13 inch baking dish with parchment paper, leaving room on the sides. Turn the dough out onto a lightly floured work surface and, using a rolling in, roll into a 15x9 inch rectangle. I used a ruler for accuracy. Make sure the dough is smooth and evenly thick, even at the corners.

For the Filling:

In a small bowl, mix together sugar and cinnamon. Spread the dough rectangle with softened butter and sprinkle generously with all the cinnamon-sugar mixture. Tightly roll up the dough and cut into 16 even rolls (1 inch in width each) with a very sharp knife. Arrange them in the prepared baking pan, cut sides up. Cover the rolls and let them rise in a warm place for about 30 minutes - 1 hour.

Preheat the oven to 375F degrees. Cover the rolls with aluminum foil and bake for about 25-30 minutes, until they are lightly golden in color. Transfer the pan to a rack to cool for about 15 minutes.

Make the Glaze:

In a small bowl, mix together all the glaze **ingredients** and drizzle over rolls before serving.

Nutrition:
- 374 Calories
- 5.8g Total fat
- 70.1g Carbohydrates

2. *Waffle with Spicy Chicken*

Preparation Time: 2 hours
Cooking Time: 10 minutes
Servings: 4

Ingredients:
Sweet Hot Maple Glaze:
- 1 cup honey
- 1 cup maple syrup
- 1 teaspoon chili powder
- 1 teaspoon paprika
- 1 teaspoon ground black pepper
- 1 teaspoon apple cider vinegar
- 1/4 teaspoon cayenne
- 1/2 teaspoon kosher salt

Waffles:
- 2 cups all-purpose flour
- 1 cup shredded sharp Cheddar
- 2 tablespoons sugar
- 2 teaspoons baking powder
- 3 to 4 scallions, chopped, whites and greens separated
- 7 to 8 dashes hot sauce
- 2 teaspoons kosher salt, plus a pinch
- 2 large eggs
- 2 cups whole milk
- 8 tablespoons (1 stick) unsalted butter, melted
- Nonstick cooking spray, for the waffle iron

Fried Chicken:
- Vegetable or canola oil, for frying
- 8 boneless, skin-on chicken thighs
- 1 cup buttermilk
- 2 cups all-purpose flour
- 1 teaspoon garlic powder
- 1 teaspoon onion powder
- 1 teaspoon paprika

- 1 teaspoon ground black pepper
- 1/2 teaspoons kosher salt, plus more for seasoning

Directions:

For the glaze: Combine the honey, maple syrup, chili powder, paprika, black pepper, vinegar, cayenne, and salt in a small saucepot. Bring just to a simmer. Remove from the heat and let steep for 20 minutes, then strain into a clean container.

For the waffles: Preheat the oven to 250 degrees F and place a rack in the middle of the oven. Place a baking sheet fitted with a wire rack in the oven.

Whisk together the flour, Cheddar, sugar, baking powder, hot sauce, scallion whites, and salt in a large bowl and set aside.

In another large bowl, whisk the eggs and a pinch of salt until just broken up, then add the milk and whisk. Pour in the melted butter and whisk until combined.

Add the wet **ingredients** to the dry **ingredients** and stir with a rubber spatula until the flour is just incorporated and no streaks remain (the batter may have a few lumps).

Preheat a Belgian waffle iron to medium heat according to the manufacturer's instructions. Spray with nonstick cooking spray, add some batter, close the lid, and cook until the steam starts to diminish (open the top and peek for doneness after a few minutes). Transfer the waffle to the wire rack in the oven to keep warm. Repeat with the remaining batter to make 8 waffles.

For the chicken: Pour 5-inches of oil in a heavy-bottomed pot. Heat over medium-high heat until a deep-frying thermometer inserted in the oil reaches 360 degrees F.

Place the chicken thighs and buttermilk in a bowl. In a separate bowl, add the flour, garlic powder, onion powder, paprika, pepper, and salt, and mix to combine. Dredge each thigh in the flour mix, then shake off any excess flour and carefully place in the oil. Fry until golden, 7 to 8 minutes. Remove the chicken to a paper bag or paper towels to drain excess grease and immediately season with salt.

Place each piece of fried chicken on top of a waffle and top each with some glaze and scallion greens to serve.

Nutrition:
- 1168 Calories
- 49.1g Total fat
- 94.7g Carbohydrates

3. Cheesecake Pancakes

Preparation Time: 10 minutes
Cooking Time: 6 minutes
Servings: 12

Ingredients:
- Pancakes
- 1 package (8 oz) cream cheese
- 2 cups Original Bisquick™ mix
- ½ cup graham cracker crumbs
- ¼ cup sugar
- 1 cup milk
- 2 eggs
- Strawberry Syrup
- 1 cup sliced fresh strawberries
- ½ cup strawberry syrup for pancakes

Directions:
Slice cream cheese lengthwise into four pieces. Place on ungreased cookie sheet; cover and freeze 8 hours or overnight. Brush griddle or skillet with vegetable oil, or spray with cooking spray; heat griddle to 375°F or heat skillet over medium heat.

Cut cream cheese into bite-size pieces; set aside. In a large bowl, stir Bisquick mix, graham cracker crumbs, sugar, milk, and eggs with whisk or fork until blended. Stir in cream cheese.

For each pancake, pour slightly less than 1/3 cup batter onto hot griddle. Cook until edges are dry. Turn; cook other sides until golden brown.

In a small bowl, mix strawberries and syrup; top pancakes with strawberry mixture.

Nutrition:
- 132 Calories
- 5.3g Total fat
- 18.7g Carbohydrates

4. Starbucks Lemon Bread

Preparation Time: 15 minutes
Cooking Time: 50 minutes
Servings: 2

Ingredients:
- 1 1/2 cups all-purpose flour
- 1/2 teaspoon baking powder
- 1/4 teaspoon baking soda
- 1/4 teaspoon salt
- 1/2 cup unsalted butter softened
- 1 cup granulated sugar
- 3 large eggs
- 1/2 teaspoon vanilla extract
- 1 teaspoon lemon extract*
- zest of 1 large lemon or use 1 and 1/2 lemons if you don't have lemon extract
- 2 tablespoons lemon juice
- 1/3 cup buttermilk sour cream works too
- Lemon Icing
- 1 cup powdered sugar add more until desired consistency is reached
- 1 tablespoon lemon juice
- 1 tablespoon cream or milk

Directions:
Lemon Loaf
Preheat the oven to 350F degrees. Grease and flour an 8 x 4-inch loaf pan, or line with parchment paper.
In a medium bowl, whisk together the flour, baking powder, baking soda & salt.
In a separate bowl, beat together the butter and sugar until fluffy - this will take at least 3 minutes.
Mix in the eggs 1 at a time. Then mix in the vanilla extract, optional lemon extract, lemon zest, and lemon juice.

With the mixer on low speed, mix in about 1/2 of the flour mixture followed by about 1/2 of the buttermilk. Turn off the mixer and scrape down the sides of the bowl.

Repeat the process with the rest of the flour mixture and buttermilk.

Pour the batter into the prepared pan and bake for 50-60 minutes. It will be done when an inserted toothpick comes out clean, and the top feels firm to the touch. If after about 30-40 minutes the top is browning too much, tent a piece of aluminum foil over top and continue baking.

Cool the loaf fully before icing (otherwise, the icing will melt through the cake and run off the sides).

Lemon Icing

In a medium bowl, whisk together the powdered sugar, lemon juice, and cream/milk until smooth. Add in more powdered sugar or cream as needed for the desired consistency.

Remove the cooled loaf from the pan and drizzle or pour over top.

Nutrition:
- 477 Calories
- 20g Total fat
- 70.8g Carbohydrates

5. Barrel Cracker French Toast

Preparation Time: 1 minute
Cooking Time: 5 minutes
Servings: 1

Ingredients:
- 8 slices Texas Toast (or Sourdough bread)
- 4 eggs
- 1 cup Milk
- 2 Tablespoons Sugar
- 4 teaspoons Vanilla extract
- 2 pinches of salt

Directions:
Whisk eggs, milk, sugar, vanilla, and salt together in a large bowl.
Heat griddle to 350 (or heat a skillet on medium heat). Grease with butter/margarine or non-stick cooking spray.
Dip each slice of bread in the egg mixture for 30 seconds on each side.
Place slices on the griddle and cook for 4-5 minutes, or until golden brown.
Serve with a pat of butter and your favorite syrup!

Nutrition:
- 1312 Calories
- 30.5g Total fat
- 191g Carbohydrates
- 54.1g Protein

6. Egg McMuffins

Preparation Time: 5 minutes
Cooking Time: 10 minutes
Servings: 2

Ingredients:
- 1 tablespoon unsalted butter (1/2 ounce; 15g), softened, divided
- 1 English muffin, split
- 1 slice high-quality Canadian bacon
- Nonstick cooking spray
- 1 large egg
- Kosher salt and freshly ground black pepper
- 1 slice American, cheddar, Swiss, or Jack cheese

Directions:
Spread 1 teaspoon butter on each half of the English muffin and place halves in a 10-inch nonstick or cast-iron skillet over medium heat. Cook, swirling muffin halves and pressing gently to get good contact with the pan, until both pieces are well browned, about 4 minutes. Transfer to a sheet of aluminum foil, split side up.

Melt remaining 1 teaspoon butter in the now-empty skillet and increase heat to medium-high. Add bacon and cook, turning frequently, until browned and crisp around the edges, about 1 1/2 minutes. Transfer bacon to lower muffin half.

Place the lid of a quart-sized, wide-mouthed Mason jar (both the lid and the sealing ring) upside down in the now-empty skillet. (The side the jar screws onto should be facing up.) Spray the inside with nonstick cooking spray and break the egg into it. Poke the egg yolk with a fork to break it and season with salt and pepper. Pour 3/4 cup (180ml) water into the skillet, cover, and cook until egg is set, about 2 minutes.

Using a thin spatula, transfer Mason jar lid to a paper

towel-lined plate. Pour excess water out of the skillet and return it to the stovetop with the heat off. Flip Mason jar lid over and gently remove it to release the egg. Place egg on top of bacon and top with cheese slice. Close sandwich, wrap in aluminum foil and return to the now-empty skillet. Let it warm up in the skillet for 2 minutes with the heat off, flipping occasionally. Unwrap and serve immediately.

Nutrition:

- 96 Calories
- 2.7g Total fat
- 12.8g Carbohydrates
- 5.3g Protein

7. Pumpkin Pancakes

Preparation Time: 10 minutes
Cooking Time: 10 minutes
Servings: 9

Ingredients:
- 1 ½ cups milk
- 1 cup pumpkin puree
- 1 egg
- 2 tablespoons vegetable oil
- 2 tablespoons vinegar
- 2 cups all-purpose flour
- 3 tablespoons brown sugar
- 2 teaspoons baking powder
- 1 teaspoon baking soda
- 1 teaspoon ground allspice
- 1 teaspoon ground cinnamon
- ½ teaspoon ground ginger
- ½ teaspoon salt

Directions:
In a bowl, mix together the milk, pumpkin, egg, oil, and vinegar. Combine the flour, brown sugar, baking powder, baking soda, allspice, cinnamon, ginger, and salt in a separate bowl. Stir into the pumpkin mixture just enough to combine.
Heat a lightly oiled griddle or frying pan over medium-high heat. Pour or scoop the batter onto the griddle, using approximately 1/4 cup for each pancake. Brown on both sides and serve hot.

Nutrition:
- 134 Calories
- 5g Total fat
- 18g Carbohydrates

8. Frittata

Preparation Time: 5 minutes
Cooking Time: 20 minutes
Servings: 6

Ingredients:
- 6 large eggs, enough to cover the ingredients
- 1/4 cup heavy cream
- 1 teaspoon kosher salt, divided
- 4 slices thick-cut bacon (8 ounces), chopped (optional)
- 2 small Yukon gold potatoes, peeled and thinly sliced
- 1/4 teaspoon freshly ground black pepper
- 2 cups baby spinach (2 ounces)
- 2 cloves garlic, minced
- 2 teaspoons fresh thyme leaves
- 1 cup shredded cheese, such as Gruyère, Fontina, or cheddar (optional)

Directions:
Heat the oven. Arrange a rack in the middle of the oven and heat to 400°F.

Whisk the eggs and cream together. Whisk the eggs, heavy cream, and 1/2 teaspoon salt together in a small bowl; set aside.

Cook the bacon. Place the bacon in a cold 10- to 12-inch nonstick oven safe frying pan or cast-iron skillet, then turn the heat to medium-high. Cook the bacon, stirring occasionally, until crisp, 8 to 10 minutes. Remove the bacon with a slotted spoon to a paper towel-lined plate and pour off all but 2 tablespoons of the fat. (If omitting the bacon, heat 2 tablespoons oil in the skillet, then proceed with adding the potatoes).

Sauté the potatoes in bacon fat. Return the pan to medium heat, add the potatoes and sprinkle with the pepper and the remaining 1/2 teaspoon salt. Cook, stirring occasionally, until tender and lightly browned, 4 to 6 minutes.

Wilt the spinach with the garlic and thyme. Pile the spinach into the pan with the garlic and thyme, and cook, stirring, for 30 seconds to 1 minute or until spinach wilts. Add the bacon back to the pan and stir to evenly distribute.

Add the cheese. Spread the vegetables into an even layer, flattening with a spatula. Sprinkle the cheese on top and let it just start to melt.

Pour the egg mixture into the skillet. Pour the egg mixture over the vegetables and cheese. Tilt the pan to make sure the eggs settle evenly over all the vegetables. Cook for a minute or two until you see the eggs at the edges of the pan beginning to set.

Bake the frittata for 8 to 10 minutes. Bake until the eggs are set, 8 to 10 minutes. To check, cut a small slit in the center of the frittata. If raw eggs run into the cut, bake for another few minutes; if the eggs are set, pull the frittata from the oven. For a browned, crispy top, run the frittata under the broiler for a minute or two at the end of cooking.

Cool and serve. Cool in the pan for 5 minutes, then slice into wedges and serve.

Nutrition:
- 324 Calories
- 25g Total fat
- 2g Carbohydrates
- 19g Protein

9. Ragout

Preparation Time: 2 minutes
Cooking Time: 15 minutes
Servings: 2

Ingredients:
- 2 tablespoons extra-virgin olive oil, divided
- 2 lb. chuck roast, cut into 2" cubes
- Kosher salt
- Freshly ground black pepper
- 1 medium yellow onion, chopped
- 5 cloves garlic, thinly sliced
- 1/2 tsp. fennel seeds
- 1/4 tsp. red pepper flakes
- 2 tablespoons tomato paste
- 1/4 c. red wine
- 1 (28 oz.) can whole peeled tomatoes
- 1/4 c. water
- 3 sprigs thyme
- 1 bay leaf
- 2 teaspoons balsamic vinegar
- Parmesan, for serving
- Freshly chopped parsley, for serving

Directions:
In a large stockpot over medium heat, heat 1 tablespoon oil. Season chuck roast with salt and pepper and sear, in batches if needed, until browned on all sides, 10 minutes. Remove into a large bowl.

Heat remaining oil, still over medium heat. Add onion and cook until soft, 6 minutes. Add garlic, fennel seeds, and red pepper flakes and cook until fragrant, 1 minute more.

Add tomato paste and cook until it is darkened in color, 1 to 2 minutes more. Deglaze the pot with wine, scraping any brown bits up at the bottom of your pot

with a wooden spoon.
Add whole peeled tomatoes, water, thyme, bay leaf, balsamic vinegar, and seared pot roast and season with salt and pepper. Stir to combine and reduce heat to low. Cover and simmer, stirring occasionally, until meat easily shreds, 2 to 2 1/2 hours. Use a wooden spoon to break up tomatoes and meat, and remove bay leaf. Serve over your favorite pasta or polenta. Top with parmesan and parsley before serving.

Nutrition:
- 180 Calories
- 14.1g Total fat
- 13.8g Carbohydrates

10. Blueberry Pancakes

Preparation Time: 5 minutes
Cooking Time: 15 minutes
Servings: 1

Ingredients:
- 2 cups all-purpose flour
- 2 tablespoons baking powder
- 1 teaspoon kosher salt
- 3 tablespoons light brown sugar
- 2 eggs
- 1 teaspoon vanilla
- 1 1/2 cups milk
- 5 tablespoons butter, melted
- 2 cups fresh blueberries
- butter for frying

Directions:
In a large bowl, whisk the flour, baking powder, salt, and brown sugar together.
In a separate bowl, whisk the eggs, vanilla, and milk together.
Add the wet ingredients into the dry and mix until just combined. Lastly, mix in the melted butter and stir until combined, the batter will be slightly lumpy. Set the batter aside while you heat your griddle to medium-low heat. Melt a small pat of butter on the griddle and then scoop out 1/4 cup of pancake batter onto the hot griddle and top evenly with blueberries, as many or few as you prefer.
Cook until the edges are set, and bubbles form on top of the pancake. Flip and cook until browned.
Serve warm.

Nutrition:
- 45 Calories
- 0.1g Total fat
- 11.9g Carbohydrates

11. Brown Sugar Bacon

Preparation Time: 5 minutes
Cooking Time: 20 minutes
Servings: 11

Ingredients:
- 1/4 cup firmly packed brown sugar
- 2 teaspoons chili powder
- 8 slices thick-cut bacon

Directions:
Preheat oven to 400 degrees F. Line a rimmed baking sheet with aluminum foil. Set a cooling rack inside the prepared pan and set aside.

In a shallow dish, combine the brown sugar and chili powder. Dredge the bacon slices in the brown sugar mixture and arrange the bacon on the rack. Bake in the preheated oven until crisp, about 20 minutes. Transfer to a serving plate and serve.

Nutrition:
- 157 Calories
- 11g Total fat
- 3g Carbohydrates
- 11g Protein

CHAPTER 2
Energizing
Smoothie Recipes

1. Jamba Juice: Protein Berry Workout

Preparation Time: 5 minutes
Cooking Time: 0 minutes
Servings: 2

Ingredients
- 1 cup vanilla soy milk
- 1 scoop vanilla protein powder, desired brand
- 1 cup frozen strawberries
- 1 frozen banana, sliced (slice before freezing)
- 1 cup ice

Directions:
Put all the ingredients and fill it to the max water line, then blend until smooth.

Nutrition:
- 418 calories
- 24g fats
- 5g fiber

2. Jamba Juice: Razzamatazz Smoothie

Preparation Time: 5 minutes
Cooking Time: 0 minutes
Servings: 2

Ingredients:
- 1 cup fresh orange juice
- ½ cup coconut yogurt
- ¼ cup shredded purple cabbage
- ½ cup frozen raspberries
- ½ cup frozen strawberries
- ½ small banana, sliced
- 2-3 ice cubes

Directions:
Put all the ingredients and fill it to the max water line, then blend until smooth.

Nutrition:
- 501 calories
- 5g fiber
- 12g protein

3. Jamba Juice: Strawberry Raspberry Banana

Preparation Time: 5 minutes
Cooking Time: 0 minutes
Servings: 2

Ingredients:
- ½ cup apple juice
- ½ cup almond milk
- ¾ cup frozen strawberries
- ½ cup fresh raspberries
- ½ small banana, sliced
- 1 cup ice

Directions:
Put all the ingredients and fill it to the max water line, then blend until smooth.

Nutrition:
- 410 calories
- 31g fats
- 6g protein

4. Jamba Juice: Strawberry Surf Rider

Preparation Time: 5 minutes
Cooking Time: 0 minutes
Servings: 2

Ingredients:
- 1 cup lemonade
- 2 tablespoons lime juice
- ½ cup non-fat frozen yogurt
- 1 cup strawberries
- 1 cup of ice cubes

Directions:
Put all the ingredients and fill it to the max water line, then blend until smooth.

Nutrition:
- 440 calories
- 29g fats
- 4g protein

5. Jamba Juice: Strawberry Whirl Smoothie

Preparation Time: 5 minutes
Cooking Time: 0 minutes
Servings: 2

Ingredients:
- 1 cup lemonade
- 2 tablespoons lime juice
- ½ cup non-fat frozen yogurt
- 1 cup strawberries
- 1 cup of ice cubes

Directions:
Put all the ingredients and fill it to the max water line, then blend until smooth.

Nutrition:
- 501 calories
- 6g fiber
- 18g fats

6. Panera Bread: Peach & Blueberry Smoothie

Preparation Time: 5 minutes
Cooking Time: 0 minutes
Servings: 2

Ingredients:
- ¼ cup frozen blueberries
- 1 small frozen peach, pitted and sliced (slice before freezing)
- ½ frozen banana, sliced (slice before freezing)
- ¾ cup unsweetened almond milk
- ½ cup fresh orange juice

Directions:
Put all the ingredients and fill it to the max water line, then blend until smooth.

Nutrition:
- 600 calories
- 19g fats
- 6g fiber

CHAPTER 3
Milk Shakes

1. Tropical Smoothie Café's Copycat Peanut Paradise

Preparation Time: 5 minutes
Cooking Time: 0 minutes
Servings: 1

Ingredients
- 2 tablespoons nonfat milk powder
- 1 tablespoon honey
- 1 medium ripe banana
- ½ cup plain yogurt
- 1 tablespoon creamy peanut butter
- 2 ice cubes

Directions
Add the ice cubes and other ingredients to a blender or food processor.
Blend for about 30 seconds until the mixture is smooth, and the ice is crushed completely. Pour into serving glass; serve chilled.

Nutrition:
- 679 calories
- 31g fats
- 7g protein

2. McDonald's Copycat Shamrock Shake

Preparation Time 5 minutes
Cooking Time: 0 minutes
Servings: 2

Ingredients
·   1¼–1½ cups vanilla ice cream
·   3 tablespoons 2% milk
·   Dash of peppermint extract or 3 tablespoons crème de menthe
·   7 thin mint cookies
·   Green food coloring (optional)

Directions
Blend all the ingredients until smooth. Pour into serving glasses; serve chilled.

Nutrition:
·   684 calories
·   34g fats
·   7.9g protein

3. Smoothie King's Copycat Caribbean Way

Preparation Time: 10 minutes
Cooking Time: 0 minutes
Servings: 4

Ingredients
- 2 cups frozen strawberries
- 1 cup orange juice
- ¾ cup strawberry-banana yogurt
- 1 medium banana, sliced and frozen

Directions
Blend all the ingredients until smooth. Pour into four serving glass; serve chilled.

Nutrition:
- 681 calories
- 36g fats
- 8g protein

CHAPTER 4
Soup Recipes

1. Ancient Grains Soup

Preparation Time: 10 minutes
Cooking Time: 45 minutes
Servings: 6

Ingredients

- 1 ¾ ounces celery, diced
- 2 ½ ounces onion, diced
- 1 teaspoon fresh parsley, chopped
- 2 ½ ounces carrot, peeled & diced
- 1 ½ ounces freekeh, cooked
- 2 teaspoon garlic, crushed (approximately 2 cloves)
- 1 can tomatoes, chopped (1 pound)
- 2 ounces amaranth, cooked
- 1 ½ ounces quinoa, cooked
- ¾ tablespoon olive oil
- 14 ounces water
- ¼ teaspoon each of pepper & salt

Directions

Over moderate heat in a medium casserole; heat the olive oil for a couple of minutes. Once hot, add & cook the onion together with celery, garlic, and carrot until for 3 to 5 minutes, until onion is translucent.

Add tomatoes (along with its accumulated juices) followed by freekeh, amaranth, quinoa & water. Increase the heat & bring the mixture to a boil. Once done, decrease the heat & let simmer for 12 to 15 more minutes, then remove the casserole from heat.

Carefully transfer the contents to a blender & add in the parsley. Purée until combined well. Season with pepper and salt. Serve hot & enjoy.

Nutrition:

- 171 calories
- 28g carbs
- 26g protein

2. Piranha Pale Ale Chili

Preparation Time: 40 minutes
Cooking Time: 40 minutes
Servings: 8

Ingredients
- 1 pound each of ground beef & ground pork
- 2 tablespoons chili powder
- 1 bottle Piranha Pale Ale (12-ounce)
- 2 cups onion, diced
- 1 teaspoon ground black pepper
- ½ teaspoon cayenne
- 1 teaspoon garlic powder
- 2 cups water
- 1 can crushed tomatoes (15-ounce)
- ½ cup all-purpose flour
- 1 teaspoon dried thyme
- 2 cans pinto beans (15-ounce, along with the liquid)
- 1 tablespoon salt

For Garnish:
- 1 cups cheddar cheese, shredded
- ½ cup sour cream
- 1 cup Monterey Jack cheese, shredded
- ½ cup green onion, chopped

Directions
Brown the ground meats over medium heat in a large saucepan. Drain any excess fat off. Add onion followed by cayenne, garlic powder, chili powder, spices, black pepper, thyme, and salt; continue to sauté for 3 to 5 more minutes.

Combine flour with water & add the mixture to the pan.

Add the leftover **ingredients** to the hot pan; bring the chili to a simmer & let simmer for 1 ½ hours, uncovered, stirring occasionally.

Serve approximately 1 ¼ cups of the prepared chili in a carved-out round of sourdough bread or in a bowl. Combine the shredded cheeses together & top the chili with approximately ¼ cup of the cheese blend followed by a tablespoon of the sour cream & garnish with a tablespoon of chopped green onions. Serve and enjoy.

Nutrition:
- 175 calories
- 30g carbs
- 24g protein

3. Chicken Tortilla Soup

Preparation Time: 10 minutes
Cooking Time: 30 minutes
Servings: 2

Ingredients
- 1 chicken breast; chopped into small pieces
- ½ cup sweet corn
- 1 cup onion, chopped
- 3 tablespoons fresh cilantro, chopped
- 1 cup chicken broth
- Avocado to taste
- 1 can diced chilies & tomatoes (8ounces)
- Colby jack cheese to taste
- 1 squirt of lime juice in an individual bowl
- Tortilla chips to taste
- 1 cup water

Directions
Over moderate heat in a large, deep pot; combine the chicken broth together with water, onion, chili, and tomatoes, corn and cilantro; bring the mixture to a boil, stirring occasionally. Add in the chicken pieces; give it a good stir, and decrease the heat to a simmer. Cook for a couple of minutes, until the chicken is cooked through. Add Tortilla chips followed by avocado & cheese to taste in serving bowls. Add soup & a squirt of lime to the bowls. Serve hot & enjoy.

Nutrition:
- 165 calories
- 34g carbs
- 22g protein

4. Tuscan Tomato Bisque

Preparation Time: 10 minutes
Cooking Time: 20 minutes
Servings: 4

Ingredients
- 4 garlic cloves, crushed
- 1 can chicken broth (14 ½ ounce), undiluted
- 2 cans no-salt-added diced tomatoes (14 ½ ounce each), undrained
- 1 teaspoon olive oil
- 4 -5 teaspoons parmesan cheese, grated
- 1 tablespoon balsamic vinegar
- 2 ½ cups 1" French bread cubes (2 ½ slices)
- 1 ½ teaspoons parsley flakes, dried
- Olive oil flavored cooking spray
- 1 teaspoon oregano, dried
- ½ teaspoon pepper

Directions
Arrange bread cubes on a baking sheet in a single layer & coat the bread lightly with the cooking spray. Bake until dry & toasted, for 8 to 10 minutes, at 400 F.
Now, over medium-low heat in large saucepan; heat the olive oil.
Once hot, add and sauté the garlic for 2 minutes.
Add the leftover **ingredients** (except grated parmesan cheese) & bring the mixture to a boil.
Decrease the heat & let simmer for 10 minutes, stirring every now and then.
Evenly divide the croutons among 4 to 5 bowls; ladle the soup over & sprinkle with the grated parmesan cheese. Serve immediately & enjoy.

Nutrition:
- 166 calories
- 31g carbs
- 22g protein

5. Broccoli Cheddar Soup

Preparation Time: 20 minutes
Cooking Time: 40 minutes
Servings: 4

Ingredients
- 6 tablespoons unsalted butter
- 1 small onion, chopped
- 2 cups half-and-half
- ¼ cup all-purpose flour
- 3 cups chicken broth, low-sodium
- ¼ teaspoon nutmeg, freshly grated
- 4 (7" each) sourdough bread boules (round loaves)
- 2 bay leaves
- 4 cups broccoli florets (1 large head)
- 2 ½ cups (approximately 8 ounces) sharp white & yellow cheddar cheese, grated, plus more for garnish
- 1 large carrot, diced
- Freshly ground pepper & kosher salt to taste

Directions
Over moderate heat in a large pot or Dutch oven; heat the butter until melted. Add and cook the onion for 3 to 5 minutes until tender. Whisk in the flour & continue to cook for 3 to 4 more minutes until turn golden. Slowly whisk in the half-and-half until completely smooth. Add the chicken broth followed by nutmeg and bay leaves, then season with pepper and salt; bring the mixture to a simmer. Once done, decrease the heat to medium-low & cook for 15 to 20 more minutes until thickened, uncovered.
In the meantime, prepare the bread bowls: Cut a circle into the top of each loaf using a sharp knife, leaving approximately 1" border all around. Remove the bread top and then hollow out the middle using your fingers

46

or with a fork, leaving a thick bread shell.

Add the carrot & broccoli to the broth mixture & let simmer for 15 to 20 minutes, until tender. Discard the bay leaves. Work in batches & carefully puree the soup in a blender until smooth. Add to the pot again.

Add the cheese to the soup & continue to whisk over medium heat until melted. If the soup appears to be too thick, feel free to add up to ¾ cup of water. Ladle into the bread bowls & garnish with cheese. Serve immediately & enjoy.

Nutrition:
- 178 calories
- 33g carbs
- 25g protein

6. Cheesy Walkabout Soup

Preparation Time: 15 minutes
Cooking Time: 50 minutes
Servings: 2
Ingredients:
- 6 tablespoons butter, divided
- 2 large sweet onions, thinly sliced
- 2 cups low sodium chicken broth
- ¼ teaspoon ground black pepper
- 2 chicken bouillon cubes
- 3 tablespoons flour
- ¼ teaspoon salt
- 1 ½ cups whole milk
- Pinch nutmeg
- ¼ cup Velveeta® cheese, cubed

Directions:
In a large pot or Dutch oven, melt half the butter over medium heat. Add the onions. Cook, stirring occasionally, until the onions are transparent but not browned.

Add the chicken broth, black pepper, and bouillon cubes. Mix well and cook on low to heat through.

In a separate saucepan, melt the remaining butter. Add the flour and salt and cook, whisking constantly, until smooth and lightly browned. Gradually whisk in the milk and cook over medium heat until it is very thick. Mix in the nutmeg.

Add the white sauce to the onion soup mixture, together with the Velveeta cubes. Stir gently over medium heat until the cheese is melted, and everything is combined.

Nutrition:
- 260 Calories
- 19g Total Fat
- 13g Carbs
- 5g Protein

CHAPTER 5
Appetizer Recipes

1. Panda Express's Veggie Spring Roll

Preparation Time: 15 minutes
Cooking Time: 5 minutes
Servings: 6-8

Ingredients:
- 4 teaspoons vegetable oil, divided
- 3 eggs, beaten
- 1 medium head cabbage, finely shredded
- ½ carrot, julienned
- 1 (8-ounce) can shredded bamboo shoots
- 1 cup dried, shredded wood ear mushroom, rehydrated
- 1-pound Chinese barbecue or roasted pork, cut into matchsticks
- ½ cup chopped Chinese yellow chives
- 1 green onion, thinly sliced
- 2½ teaspoons soy sauce
- 1 teaspoon salt
- 1 teaspoon sugar
- 1 (14-ounce) package egg roll wrappers
- 1 egg white, beaten
- 1-quart oil for frying, or as needed

Directions:
In a large skillet, heat 1 tablespoon of oil over medium-high heat.

When the skillet is hot, add the beaten eggs and cook until firm, then flip and cook a bit longer like an omelet. When set, remove from the pan. Cut into strips and set aside.

Add the remaining oil to the skillet and heat. When hot, add the cabbage and carrot and cook for a couple of minutes until they start to soften. Then add the bamboo shoots, mushrooms, pork, green onions, chives, soy sauce, salt, and sugar. Cook until the veggies are soft, then stir in the egg. Transfer the mixture to a bowl and refrigerate for about 1 hour.

When cooled, add about 2–3 tablespoons of filling to each egg roll wrapper. Brush some beaten egg around the edges of the wrapper and roll up, tucking in the ends first.

When all the wrappers are filled, heat about 6 inches of oil to 350°F in a deep saucepan, Dutch oven or fryer. Add the egg rolls to the hot oil a couple at a time. When golden brown and crispy, remove from oil to a paper-towel-lined plate to drain.

Serve with chili sauce or sweet and sour sauce.

Nutrition:
- 132 Calories
- 3.3g Fat
- 5.5g Carbs
- 32g Protein

2. PF Chang's Hot and Sour Soup

Preparation Time: 10 minutes
Cooking Time: 10 minutes
Servings: 4-6

Ingredients:
- 6 ounces chicken breasts, cut into thin strips
- 1-quart chicken stock
- 1 cup soy sauce
- 1 teaspoon white pepper
- 1 (6 ounces) can bamboo shoots, cut into strips
- 6 ounces wood ear mushrooms
- ½ cup cornstarch
- ½ cup water
- 2 eggs, beaten
- ½ cup white vinegar
- 6 ounces silken tofu, cut into strips
- Sliced green onions for garnish

Directions:
Cook the chicken strips in a hot skillet until cooked through. Set aside.

Add the chicken stock, soy sauce, pepper, and bamboo shoots to a stockpot and bring to a boil. Stir in the chicken and let cook for about 3–4 minutes.

In a small dish, make a slurry with the cornstarch and water. Add a bit at a time to the stockpot until the broth thickens to your desired consistency.

Stir in the beaten eggs and cook for about 45 seconds or until the eggs are done.

Remove from the heat and add the vinegar and tofu. Garnish with sliced green onions.

Nutrition:
- 345 Calories
- 1.2g Fat
- 2.2g Carbs
- 23.3g Protein

3. PF Chang's Lettuce Wraps

Preparation Time: 10 minutes
Cooking Time: 10 minutes
Servings: 4

Ingredients:
- 1 tablespoon olive oil
- 1-pound ground chicken
- 2 cloves garlic, minced
- 1 onion, diced
- ¼ cup hoisin sauce
- 2 tablespoons soy sauce
- 1 tablespoon rice wine vinegar
- 1 tablespoon ginger, freshly grated
- 1 tablespoon Sriracha (optional)
- 1 (8-ounce) can whole water chestnuts, drained and diced
- 2 green onions, thinly sliced
- Kosher salt and freshly ground black pepper to taste
- 1 head iceberg lettuce

Directions:
Add the oil to a deep skillet or saucepan and heat over medium-high heat. When hot, add the chicken and cook until it is completely cooked through. Stir while cooking to make sure it is properly crumbled.

Drain any excess fat from the skillet, then add the garlic, onion, hoisin sauce, soy sauce, ginger, sriracha, and vinegar. Cook until the onions have softened, then stir in the water chestnuts and green onion and cook for another minute or so. Add salt and pepper to taste.

Serve with lettuce leaves and eat by wrapping them up like a taco.

Nutrition:
- 156 Calories
- 4.3g Fat
- 3.7g Carbs
- 27g Protein

4. PF Chang's Shrimp Dumplings

Preparation Time: 20 minutes
Cooking Time: 10 minutes
Servings: 4-6

Ingredients:
- 1-pound medium shrimp, peeled, deveined, washed and dried, divided
- 2 tablespoons carrot, finely minced
- 2 tablespoons green onion, finely minced
- 1 teaspoon ginger, freshly minced
- 2 tablespoons oyster sauce
- ¼ teaspoon sesame oil
- 1 package wonton wrappers

Sauce
- 1 cup soy sauce
- 2 tablespoons white vinegar
- ½ teaspoon chili paste
- 2 tablespoons granulated sugar
- ½ teaspoon ginger, freshly minced
- Sesame oil to taste
- 1 cup water
- 1 tablespoon cilantro leaves

Directions:
In a food processor or blender, finely mince ½ pound of the shrimp.
Dice the other ½ pound of shrimp.
In a mixing bowl, combine both the minced and diced shrimp with the remaining **ingredients**.
Spoon about 1 teaspoon of the mixture into each wonton wrapper. Wet the edges of the wrapper with your finger, then fold up and seal tightly.
Cover and refrigerate for at least an hour.
In a medium bowl, combine all the **ingredients** for the sauce and stir until well combined.

When ready to serve, boil water in a saucepan and cover with a steamer. You may want to lightly oil the steamer to keep the dumplings from sticking. Steam the dumplings for 7–10 minutes.
Serve with sauce.

Nutrition:
- 244 Calories
- 20g Fat
- 57g Carbs
- 63g Protein

5. PF Chang's Spicy Chicken Noodle

Preparation Time: 15 minutes
Cooking Time: 15 minutes
Servings: 4-6

Ingredients:
- 2 quarts chicken stock
- 1 tablespoon granulated sugar
- 3 tablespoons white vinegar
- 2 cloves garlic, minced
- 1 tablespoon ginger, freshly minced
- ¼ cup soy sauce
- Sriracha sauce to taste
- Red pepper flakes to taste
- 1-pound boneless chicken breast, cut into thin 2–3-inch pieces
- 3 tablespoons cornstarch
- Salt to taste
- 1 cup mushrooms, sliced
- 1 cup grape tomatoes, halved
- 3 green onions, sliced
- 2 tablespoons fresh cilantro, chopped
- ½ pound pasta, cooked to just under package directions and drained

Directions:
Add the chicken stock, sugar, vinegar, garlic, ginger, soy sauce, Sriracha and red pepper flakes to a large saucepan. Bring to a boil, then lower the heat to a simmer. Let cook for 5 minutes.

Season chicken with salt to taste. In a resealable bag, combine the chicken and the cornstarch. Shake to coat.

Add the chicken to the simmering broth a piece at a time. Then add the mushrooms. Continue to cook for another 5 minutes.

Stir in the tomatoes, green onions, cilantro, and cooked pasta.
Serve with additional cilantro.

Nutrition:
· 100 Calories
· 3.7g Fat
· 6.7g Carbs
· 48g Protein

6. Pei Wei's Thai Chicken Satay

Preparation Time: 20 minutes
Cooking Time: 10-20 minutes
Servings: 2-4

Ingredients:
- 1-pound boneless, skinless chicken thighs
- 6-inch bamboo skewers, soaked in water
- Thai satay marinade
- 1 tablespoon coriander seeds
- 1 teaspoon cumin seeds
- 2 teaspoons chopped lemongrass
- 1 teaspoon salt
- 1 teaspoon turmeric powder
- ¼ teaspoon roasted chili
- ½ cup coconut milk
- 1½ tablespoons light brown sugar
- 1 teaspoon lime juice
- 2 teaspoons fish sauce
- Peanut sauce
- 2 tablespoons soy sauce
- 1 tablespoon rice wine vinegar
- 2 tablespoons brown sugar
- ¼ cup peanut butter
- 1 teaspoon chipotle Tabasco
- Thai sweet cucumber relish
- ¼ cup white vinegar
- ¾ cup sugar
- ¾ cup water
- 1 tablespoon ginger, minced
- 1 Thai red chili, minced
- 1 medium cucumber
- 1 tablespoon toasted peanuts, chopped

Directions:

Cut any excess fat from the chicken, then cut into strips about 3 inches long and 1 inch wide. Thread the strips onto the skewers.

Prepare the Thai Satay Marinade and the Peanut Sauce in separate bowls by simply whisking together all the ingredients for each.

Dip the chicken skewers in the Thai Satay Marinade and marinate for at least 4 hours. Reserve the marinade when you remove the chicken skewers.

You can cook the skewers on the grill, basting with the marinade halfway through, or you can do the same in a 350-degree F oven. They taste better on the grill.

To prepare the Cucumber Relish, simply add all the **ingredients** together and stir to make sure the cucumber is coated.

Peanut sauce:

Whisk all **ingredients** until well incorporated. Store in an airtight container in the refrigerator. It will last for 3 days.

When the chicken skewers are done cooking, serve with peanut sauce and the cucumber relish.

Nutrition:

- 298 Calories
- 5.4g Fat
- 7.5g Carbs
- 61g Protein

7. Chicken Lettuce Wraps

Preparation Time: 5 minutes
Cooking Time: 25 minutes
Servings: 2

Ingredients
- 2 chicken breasts, boneless skinless
- 2/3 cup mushroom
- 4 -5 leaves of iceberg lettuce
- 1 teaspoon garlic, minced
- 3 tablespoons onions, chopped
- 1 cup water chestnut
- 3 tablespoons oil

For Stir Fry Sauce
- 2 tablespoons brown sugar
- ½ teaspoon rice wine vinegar
- 2 tablespoons soy sauce

For Special Sauce
- 2 tablespoons rice wine vinegar
- 1 -2 teaspoon red chili & garlic paste
- ¼ cup sugar
- 1 tablespoon lemon juice
- 2 tablespoons soy sauce
- 1 tablespoon hot mustard
- 2 tablespoons ketchup
- 1/8 teaspoon sesame oil
- ½ cup plus 2 teaspoons water

Directions
Dissolve sugar with water in a small sized bowl. Add in the rice wine vinegar, soy sauce, ketchup, sesame oil & lemon juice; mix well & prepare the special sauce; cover & let refrigerate until ready to serve.
Now, combine hot mustard with hot water; set aside. To pour over the wraps, add in the garlic chili & mustard sauce in the end to the special sauce mixture.

Over high heat in a large frying pan or wok; heat the oil & sauté the chicken breasts until done, for 4 to 5 minutes on each side. Remove the chicken pieces from the heat & let cool at room temperature for a couple of minutes.

Don't remove the oil; keep it in the pan & try to keep it hot. In the meantime, mince the mushrooms and water chestnuts to the size of small peas.

Now, make the stir fry sauce: In a small bowl, mix soy sauce together with rice vinegar & brown sugar; mix well. When you can handle the chicken easily and once cool, mince it as the water chestnuts and mushrooms are. Add a tablespoon of vegetable oil more to the pan & add in the garlic, chicken, onions, mushrooms & water chestnuts to the hot pan. Add in the stir fry sauce, sauté the mixture for a couple of minutes, then serve in the lettuce leaves.

Nutrition:
- 287 calories
- 6.9g carbs
- 59g protein

8. BBQ Spare Ribs

Preparation Time: 15 minutes
Cooking Time: 5 hours and 35 minutes
Servings: 6

Ingredients
For the Marinade:
- 2 racks pork spareribs (4 to 5 pounds)
- 2 tablespoons apple cider vinegar
- 1 garlic clove, minced
- ¼ cup light brown sugar, packed
- 2 tablespoons onion, minced
- Freshly ground black pepper & kosher salt

For the Barbecue Sauce:
- 2 tablespoons Worcestershire sauce
- ½ teaspoon liquid smoke
- 3 garlic cloves, smashed
- ¼ cup tomato paste
- 2 tablespoons vegetable oil
- 1 ¾ cups apple cider vinegar
- 1 tablespoon honey
- ¼ cup molasses
- 1 cup pineapple preserves
- 2 teaspoons instant espresso powder
- 1 tablespoon mustard powder
- Freshly ground black pepper
- 1 cup ketchup
- ½ teaspoon cayenne pepper

For the Rub:
- 1 tablespoon onion powder
- 1 teaspoon each celery salt & celery seeds
- ½ cup light brown sugar, packed
- 1 tablespoon chili powder
- ¼ teaspoon cayenne pepper
- 1 tablespoon garlic powder

Directions

First, prepare the marinade: In a large bowl, whisk vinegar together with the onion, brown sugar, garlic, ½ teaspoon black pepper & 1 tablespoon salt; whisk well. Place the ribs on a large cutting board, meat-side down. Begin with one end; slip a paring knife just under the membrane & loosen it with the knife and then pull it off. Coat both sides of the ribs with the prepared marinade; wrap the meat pieces in a plastic wrap & let refrigerate for overnight.

Now, prepare the rub: In a separate medium-sized bowl, mix the chili powder together with brown sugar, onion powder, garlic powder, celery seeds & celery salt, cayenne, 1 teaspoon black pepper & 1 tablespoon salt; mix well.

Soak approximately 2 cups of the hickory wood chips in water for a minimum period of half an hour, before you use them. In the meantime, preheat your grill over medium-low heat & prepare it for indirect grilling. Cover the grill's cooler side grate with foil.

Drain the wood chips & scatter them on top of the hot coals. Close the lid & let the smoke to build up for a minimum period of 10 minutes. Rinse the meat and remove the marinade from the ribs; pat them dry using paper towels. Rub both sides of the meat with the spice mixture using your hands.

Place the coated ribs on foil & over indirect heat, meat-side up. Close the lid; cook for approximately 1 hour & 30 minutes, until the meat slightly shrinks back & you can see a bit of bone, undisturbed.

Rotate (keep them over indirect heat and meat-side up), close the lid & continue to cook for 2 hours or a little longer; maintain the temperature of your grill by adding more of hot coals.

In the meantime, prepare the barbecue sauce: Over medium heat settings in a medium-sized saucepan; heat the vegetable oil. Once hot, cook the garlic for a minute, until golden, stirring occasionally. Stir in the chili powder and tomato paste for a minute, until well incorporated. Whisk in Worcestershire sauce, ¼ cup water, vinegar, the molasses, espresso powder, mustard powder, honey, cayenne, and ¾ teaspoon black pepper. Bring everything to a simmer & cook for 5 minutes, whisking occasionally.

Whisk in the pineapple preserves and ketchup. Bring to a moderate simmer & cook for 40 to 45 minutes, until thickened, whisking every now and then. Whisk in the liquid smoke & allow the sauce cool for a couple of minutes at room temperature & then take off the garlic.

Generously baste the ribs with this barbecue sauce. Close the lid; continue to cook for 20 more minutes until glazed. Transfer the meat to a large cutting board & let rest for a couple of minutes before cutting the meat into individual ribs.

Serve the cooked ribs with some more sauce & enjoy.

Nutrition:
- 279 calories
- 5.9g carbs
- 57g protein

9. Buddha's Feast Vegetable Stir-Fry

Preparation Time: 15 minutes
Cooking Time: 15 minutes
Servings: 10

Ingredients

- 12 ounces broccoli, florets
- ½ cup Vegetable Stock, Homemade or canned vegetable broth, low-sodium
- 8 ounces shiitake, small or white mushrooms, stemmed & julienned
- 1 can sliced water chestnuts, drained (8 ounces)
- 2 tablespoons cornstarch
- 1 teaspoon Chinese chili paste
- 3 tablespoons soy sauce, low-sodium
- 1 tablespoon mirin
- 8 ounces firm tofu, cut into ½" cubes
- ½ head bok choy cut into 1-inch dice
- 2 garlic cloves, minced
- 1 can baby corn, drained (14 ounces)
- 4 carrots, peeled & sliced thinly on the diagonal
- Nonstick cooking spray
- Cooked brown rice, for serving

Directions

Whisk stock together with cornstarch, soy sauce, chili paste & mirin in a small-sized bowl. Place half cup of the mixture in a small bowl and then add in the tofu; let sit for half an hour at room temperature. Reserve the leftover sauce. Fill ice water in a large bowl; set aside.

Fill a large pot with water & bring it to a boil over moderate heat settings. Cook the bok choy in boiling water for a couple of minutes. Transfer them to ice water using a large slotted spoon. Once cool down; remove them from the ice water; set them aside. Cook broccoli florets for a minute in the same pot. Transfer them to the ice water to cool as well. Remove & place them into the bowl with the bok choy; set aside.

Place the tofu on paper towels to drain, try keeping the sauce. Lightly coat a large skillet or wok with the cooking spray & heat it over medium heat settings. Add in the mushrooms & carrots; cook for a couple of minutes, stirring every now and then. Add in the broccoli, bok choy, tofu, baby corn, water chestnuts, & garlic. Cook for an additional minute or two. Add in the reserved sauce; cook for a couple of more minutes, until it thickens; stirring frequently. Serve immediately with some hot cooked brown rice.

Nutrition:
- 280 calories
- 6g carbs
- 54g protein

CHAPTER 6
Old and Modern
Sauce & Dressing
Recipes

1. Rondelé Garlic & Herbs Cheese Spread

Preparation Time: 5 minutes
Cooking Time: 0 minutes
Servings: 4

Ingredients
- 18 ounces cream cheese, whipped
- 2 teaspoons fresh garlic, finely minced
- 1 teaspoon Italian seasoning
- ½ teaspoon salt
- ¼ teaspoon onion powder
- Sliced green onions for garnish

Directions
Combine all the ingredients in a bowl and then transfer to a glass jar. Refrigerate for a few hours before serving and sprinkle with sliced green onions.

Nutrition
- 451 Calories
- 44g total fat
- 4.1g carbs
- 9.7g Protein

2. Lipton Onion Soup Mix

Preparation Time: 5 minutes
Cooking Time: 0 minutes
Servings: 4

Ingredients
- 1½ cups dry onion flakes
- ½ cup beef bouillon powder
- 8 teaspoons onion powder
- ½ teaspoon crushed celery seeds
- ½ teaspoon dry parsley
- ½ teaspoon sugar

Directions
Combine all ingredients in a jar. Store it with an airtight cover.

Nutrition
- 19 Calories
- 0.4g total fat
- 4.2g carbs

3. Lawry's Taco Seasonings

Preparation Time: 10 minutes
Cooking Time: 0 minutes
Servings: 2

Ingredients
- 2 tablespoons flour
- 2 teaspoons red chili powder
- 2 teaspoons paprika
- 1½ teaspoons salt, or to taste
- 1½ teaspoons onion powder
- 1 teaspoon cumin
- ½ teaspoon cayenne pepper
- ½ teaspoon garlic powder
- ½ teaspoon white sugar
- ¼ teaspoon oregano, ground

Directions
Combine all the spices in a bowl and store in a glass jar.

Nutrition
- 1 Calorie
- 0.3g total fat
- 3.1g carbs
- 0.5g Protein

4. Mrs. Dash Salt-Free Seasoning Mix

Preparation Time: 5 minutes
Cooking Time: 0 minutes
Servings: 2

Ingredients
- 2 teaspoons onion powder
- 2 teaspoons black pepper
- 2 teaspoons parsley
- 2 teaspoons dry celery seed
- 1 teaspoon dry basil
- 1 teaspoon dry bay leaf
- 2 teaspoons marjoram
- 2 teaspoons oregano
- 2 teaspoons savory
- 2 teaspoons thyme
- 2 teaspoons cayenne pepper
- 1 teaspoon coriander
- 2 teaspoons cumin
- 1 teaspoon mustard powder
- 2 teaspoons rosemary
- 2 teaspoons garlic powder
- 1 teaspoon mace

Directions
Combine all the spices in a bowl and store in a glass jar. Keep it dry.

Nutrition
- 23 Calories
- 0.8g total fat
- 4g carbs
- 0.9g Protein

5. Old Bay Seasoning

Preparation Time: 4 minutes
Cooking Time: 0 minutes
Servings: 4

Ingredients
- ¼ cup bay leaf powder
- ¼ cup celery salt
- 2 tablespoons dry mustard
- 4 teaspoons black pepper, ground
- 4 teaspoons ginger, ground
- 4 teaspoons paprika, smoked
- 2 teaspoons white pepper, ground
- 2 Teaspoons nutmeg, ground
- 2 teaspoons cloves, ground
- 2 teaspoons allspice, ground
- 1 teaspoon crushed red pepper flakes
- 1 teaspoon mace, ground
- 1 teaspoon cardamom, ground
- ½ teaspoon cinnamon, ground

Directions
Combine all the spices in a bowl and store in a glass jar. Keep it dry.

Nutrition
- 16 Calories
- 0.7g total fat
- 2.5g carbs
- 0.6g Protein

6. Lawry's Seasoned Salt

Preparation Time: 5 minutes
Cooking Time: 0 minutes
Servings: 1

Ingredients
- 1 tablespoon salt, or to taste
- 2 teaspoons white sugar
- ¼ teaspoon smoked paprika
- ¼ teaspoon turmeric powder
- ¼ teaspoon onion powder
- ¼ teaspoon garlic powder
- ¼ teaspoon cornstarch

Directions
Combine all the spices in a bowl and store in a glass jar. Keep it dry.

Nutrition
- 360mg sodium

7. Kraft Stove Top Stuffing Mix

Preparation Time: 5 minutes
Cooking Time: 10 minutes
Servings: 8

Ingredients
- 6 cups bread, cut into cubes
- 1 tablespoon parsley, flakes
- 3–4 bouillon cubes, chicken
- ¼ cup onion flakes, dried
- ½ cup celery flakes, dried
- 1 teaspoon thyme, dry
- 1 teaspoon black pepper
- ½ teaspoon sage
- ½ teaspoon salt

Directions
Preheat oven to 375°F. Bake the bread in the oven for 10 minutes. Once cool, dump all the ingredients in a bowl. Shake well to combine.
Tip: To use the prepared mixture, mix 2 cups mixture with ½ cup water and 2 tablespoons melted butter.

Nutrition
- 57 Calories
- 0.7g total fat
- 9.3g carbs
- 2.9g Protein

8. Chick-Fil-A Sauce

Preparation Time: 5 minutes
Cooking Time: 0 minutess
Servings: 4

Ingredients
- ¼ teaspoon onion powder
- ¼ teaspoon garlic salt
- ½ tablespoon yellow mustard
- ¼ teaspoon smoked paprika
- ½ tablespoon stevia extract, powdered
- 1 teaspoon liquid smoke
- ½ cup mayonnaise

Directions
Plug in a food processor, add all the ingredients in it, cover with the lid and then pulse for 30 seconds until smooth.
Tip the sauce into a bowl and then serve.

Nutrition:
- 183 Calories
- 20 g Fats

9. *Burger Sauce*

Preparation Time: 5 minutes
Cooking Time: 0 minutes
 Servings: 12

Ingredients
- 1 tablespoon chopped gherkin
- ½ teaspoon chopped dill
- ¾ teaspoon onion powder
- ¾ teaspoon garlic powder
- 1/8 teaspoon ground white pepper
- 1 teaspoon mustard powder
- ½ teaspoon erythritol sweetener
- ¼ teaspoon sweet paprika
- 1 teaspoon white vinegar
- ½ cup mayonnaise

Directions
Take a medium bowl, place all the ingredients for the sauce in it and then stir until well mixed.
Place the sauce for a minimum of overnight in the refrigerator to develop flavors and then serve with burgers.

Nutrition:
- 15 Calories
- 7 g Fats

CHAPTER 7
OLD AND MODERN LUNCH & DINNER RECIPES

1. Chicken Alfredo

Preparation Time: 10 minutes
Cooking Time: 10 minutes
Servings: 4

Ingredients
- ¾ pound fettuccine pasta
- 2 tablespoons olive oil
- ½ cup + 2 tablespoons butter (divided)
- 2 boneless skinless chicken breasts
- 1½ teaspoons salt (divided)
- 1½ teaspoons fresh ground pepper (divided)
- 3 cloves garlic, very finely chopped
- 1½ tablespoons flour
- 2 cups heavy cream
- ¾ cup grated parmesan, plus more for topping if desired
- 2 tablespoons parsley, chopped (optional, for garnish)

Directions
Cook pasta according to package instructions. Drain and set aside. Heat oil in a cast iron grill pan over high heat. Add 2 tablespoons of butter to the pan and then add the chicken breasts. Season the chicken breasts with 1 teaspoon of salt and pepper.

Cook the first side until golden brown. Flip, cover the pan, and reduce the heat to medium. Cook until the chicken is cooked thoroughly. Set aside and cover in foil. Once cooled, cut into strips.

Melt the remaining butter over medium heat in a large, deep skillet. Add garlic and cook for about 30 seconds. Reduce to medium-low heat and season with remaining salt and pepper. Add flour, whisking constantly to break up any chunks. Slowly pour the cream into the mixture. Cook until sauce is slightly thickened.

Stir in the parmesan until smooth. Remove from heat and set aside. Serve by tossing the pasta with the alfredo sauce. Place chicken on top and garnish with fresh parsley and parmesan, if desired.

Nutrition:
- 431 calories
- 6g carbs
- 35g protein

2. Parmesan Crusted Chicken

Preparation Time: 15 minutes
Cooking Time: 40 minutes
Servings: 4

Ingredients
Breading
- 1 cup plain breadcrumbs
- 2 tablespoons flour
- ¼ cup grated parmesan cheese

For dipping
- 1 cup milk

Chicken
- 2 chicken breasts
- Vegetable oil for frying
- 2 cups cooked linguini pasta
- 2 tablespoons butter
- 3 tablespoons olive oil
- 2 teaspoons crushed garlic
- ½ cup white wine
- ¼ cup water
- 2 tablespoons flour
- ¾ cup half-and-half
- ¼ cup sour cream
- ½ teaspoon salt
- 1 teaspoon fresh flat leave parsley, finely diced¾ cup mild Asiago cheese, finely grated

Garnish
- 1 Roma tomato, diced
- Grated parmesan cheese
- Fresh flat-leaf parsley, finely chopped

Directions
Pound the chicken until it flattens to ½ inch thick. Mix the breading **ingredients** in one shallow bowl and place the milk in another. Heat some oil over medium

to medium-to-low heat.

Dip the chicken in the breading, then the milk, then the breading again. Immediately place into the heated oil. Cook the chicken in the oil until golden brown, about 3-4 minutes per side. Remove the chicken and set aside on a plate lined with paper towels.

Create a roux by adding flour to heated olive oil and butter over medium heat. When the roux is done, add the garlic, water, and salt to the pan and stir. Add the wine and continue stirring and cooking.

Add the half-and-half and sour cream and stir some more. Add the cheese and let it melt. Finally, add in the parsley and remove from heat. Add pasta and stir to coat.

Divide the hot pasta between serving plates. Top each dish with the chicken, diced tomatoes, and parmesan cheese before serving.

Nutrition:
- 481 calories
- 7.6g carbs
- 31g protein

3. Chicken Giardino

Preparation Time: 10 minutes
Cooking Time: 20 minutes
Servings: 4

Ingredients
Sauce
- 1 tablespoon butter
- ¼ teaspoon dried thyme
- ½ teaspoon fresh rosemary, finely chopped
- 1 teaspoon garlic pepper seasoning
- 1 tablespoon cornstarch
- ¼ cup chicken broth
- ¼ cup water
- ¼ cup white wine
- 1 tablespoon milk
- 1 teaspoon lemon juice
- Salt and pepper

Chicken
- 2 pounds boneless skinless chicken breasts
- ¼ cup extra virgin olive oil
- 2 small rosemary sprigs
- 1 clove garlic, finely minced
- Juice of ½ lemon
- Vegetables
- ¼ cup extra-virgin olive oil
- ½ bunch fresh asparagus (remove the bottom inch of stem, cut the remainder into 1-inch pieces)
- 1 zucchini, julienned
- 1 summer squash, julienned
- 2 roma tomatoes, cut into ½-inch pieces
- ½ red bell pepper, julienned
- 1 cup broccoli florets, blanched
- ½ cup frozen peas
- 1 cup spinach, cut into ½-inch pieces
- ½ cup carrot, julienned

- 1-pound farfalle pasta (bow ties)

Directions
In a saucepan, melt the butter over medium heat. Add the thyme, garlic, pepper, and rosemary. Whisk together and cook for 1 minute. In a mixing bowl, mix together the chicken broth, water, wine, milk, and lemon juice. Slowly pour in the cornstarch and whisk constantly until it has dissolved.
Pour the mixture into the saucepan. Whisk well and then bring to a boil. Season with salt and pepper to taste, then remove from heat.
Prepare the chicken by cutting into strips width-wise. In a mixing bowl, combine the olive oil, rosemary, garlic, and lemon juice. Marinate the chicken for at least 30 minutes.
Heat ¼ cup of olive oil over medium-high heat in a saucepan. Cook the chicken strips until the internal temperature is 165°F. Add the vegetables to the saucepan and sauté until cooked. Prepare the pasta according to package instructions. Drain. Add the pasta and pasta sauce to the sauté pan.
Toss to thoroughly coat pasta and chicken in sauce. Serve.

Nutrition:
- 481 calories
- 6.5g carbs
- 30g protein

4. *Chicken and Sausage Mixed Grill*

Preparation Time: 10 minutes
Cooking Time: 35 minutes
Servings: 4

Ingredients
Marinade
- 2 teaspoons red pepper oil
- 2 tablespoons fresh rosemary, chopped
- ½ cup fresh lemon juice
- 1 teaspoon salt
- 3 bay leaves, broken into pieces
- 2 large garlic cloves, pressed
- ¼ cup extra-virgin olive oil
- Freshly shredded parmesan cheese, for serving

Skewers
- 2 pounds skinless, boneless chicken breasts
- 1-pound Italian sausage links, mild
- 1-pint cherry tomatoes
- 1 bag bamboo skewers, soaked in water for at least 30 minutes
- 3 lemons, halved
- 2 rosemary sprigs

Directions
To make the marinade, mix pepper oil, rosemary, lemon juice, salt, bay leaves, and pressed garlic in a baking dish. Cut the chicken breasts in half lengthwise. Pierce each chicken piece with a skewer and thread through. Add a cherry tomato at the end of the skewer. Coat each skewer with the marinade. Marinate for at least 3 hours in the refrigerator.

Preheat oven to 350°F. Bake sausage for 20 minutes. Let cool, then cut into 3 pieces. Grill chicken until completely cooked. Place sausages on skewers. Grill. Serve by garnishing with rosemary, lemon, and cherry tomatoes on a platter. Sprinkle with freshly shredded parmesan, if desired.

Nutrition:
- 469 calories
- 7g carbs
- 32g protein

5. Chicken Gnocchi Veronese

Preparation Time: 20 minutes
Cooking Time: 25 minutes
Servings: 4

Ingredients
- ¼ cup extra-virgin olive oil
- 1 small vidalia onion, chopped
- 1 red bell pepper, julienned
- ½ zucchini, julienned
- Salt to taste
- 4 chicken breasts, sliced it in ½-inch strips
- 2 small sprigs rosemary
- 1 glove garlic, minced
- Juice of ½ lemon

Veronese Sauce
- 1 cup parmesan cheese, grated
- ½ cup ricotta cheese
- 14 ounces heavy cream

Gnocchi
- 2 quarts water
- 1⅓ cups all-purpose flour
- 2 eggs
- 2 pounds russet potatoes
- 2 teaspoons salt
- or
- 1-pound gnocchi (potato dumplings), cooked according to package directions

Directions
If using pre-made gnocchi, cook according to package instructions. If not, begin by washing potatoes and placing them in water. Cook potatoes until soft. Remove water and cool into the refrigerator. Once cooled, peel and push potatoes through a fine grater or rice grater.

In a mixing bowl, mix the potatoes and eggs. Slowly add flour until the dough does not stick to your hands. Divide dough into four. Roll each section into a long rope. Cut into ½-inch pieces, then create impressions by gently pushing a fork into the gnocchi.

Pour water into a pot and bring to a boil. Add gnocchi and cook until they begin to float. In a mixing bowl, mix the garlic, lemon juice, rosemary, and chicken slices. Marinate for 2 hours. In another bowl, mix the parmesan cheese, ricotta cheese, and heavy cream.

Heat the olive oil in a sauté pan over medium-high heat. Add the onion, bell peppers, and zucchini. Sauté until the onion is translucent. Add the chicken to the sauté pan and cook until brown. Reduce heat and add the sauce. Simmer. Add the gnocchi and toss to coat in the sauce. Serve with additional parmesan cheese, if desired.

Nutrition:
- 521 calories
- 5.9g carbs
- 31g protein

6. Chicken Parmigiana

Preparation Time: 20 minutes
Cooking Time: 25 minutes
Servings: 4

Ingredients
· 4 boneless, skinless chicken breasts (½ pound each)
· 2 cups flour
· ½ quart milk
· 4 eggs
· 3 cups Italian breadcrumbs
· ½ cup marinara sauce
· 1 cup mozzarella cheese
· ½ cup vegetable oil
· Parsley (to garnish)
· Cooked pasta with marinara sauce to serve

Directions
Put flour in a bowl. In another bowl, mix milk and eggs together. In a third bowl, place breadcrumbs. Place chicken breasts between plastic wrap and pound to about ¼ inch in thickness. Season with salt and pepper.

Place chicken in flour, coating all sides. Dip into egg wash, then bread crumbs, coating each side evenly. Preheat oven to broil. In a cast iron pan, heat oil over medium heat. Fry each side of the chicken for 5 minutes or until golden brown. Drain on paper towels. Place chicken on a baking dish. Top with marinara sauce and mozzarella cheese. Place in oven until cheese is melted. Garnish with parsley. Serve with a side of marinara pasta, if desired.

Nutrition:
· 489 calories
· 6.7g carbs
· 34g protein

7. Chicken and Shrimp Carbonara

Preparation Time: 35 minutes
Cooking Time: 40 minutes
Servings: 8

Ingredients
Shrimp Marinade
- ¼ cup extra virgin olive oil
- ½ cup water
- 2 teaspoons Italian seasoning
- 1 tablespoon minced garlic

Chicken
- 4 boneless and skinless chicken breasts cubed
- 1 egg mixed with 1 tablespoon cold water
- ½ cup panko bread crumbs
- ½ cup all-purpose flour
- ½ teaspoon salt
- ½ teaspoon black pepper
- 2 tablespoons olive oil

Carbonara sauce
- ½ cup butter (1 stick)
- 3 tablespoons all-purpose flour
- ½ cup parmesan cheese, grated
- 2 cups heavy cream
- 2 cups milk
- 8 Canadian bacon slices, diced finely
- ¾ cup roasted red peppers, diced

Pasta
- 1 teaspoon salt
- 14 ounces spaghetti or bucatini pasta (1 package)
- Water to cook the pasta
- Shrimp
- ½ pound fresh medium shrimp, deveined and peeled
- 1-2 tablespoons olive oil for cooking

Directions

Mix all the marinade **ingredients** together in a re-sealable container or bag and add the shrimp. Refrigerate for at least 30 minutes.

To make the chicken, mix the flour, salt, pepper, and panko bread crumbs into a shallow dish. Whisk the egg with 1 tablespoon of cold water in a second shallow dish. Dip the chicken into the breadcrumb mix and after in the egg wash, and again in the breadcrumb mix. Place on a plate and let rest until all the chicken is prepared.

Warm the olive oil over medium heat in a deep, large skillet. Working in batches, add the chicken. Cook for 4 to 6 minutes per side or until the chicken is cooked through. Place the cooked chicken tenders on a plate lined with paper towels to absorb excess oil.

To make the pasta, add water to a large pot and bring to a boil. Add salt and cook the pasta according to package instructions about 10-15 minutes before the sauce is ready.

To make the shrimp, while the pasta is cooking, add olive oil to a skillet. Remove the shrimp from the marinade and shake off the excess marinade. Cook the shrimp until they turn pink, about 2-3 minutes.

To make the Carbonara sauce, in a large deep skillet, sauté the Canadian bacon with a bit of butter for 3-4 minutes over medium heat or until the bacon starts to caramelize. Add the garlic and sauté for 1 more minute. Remove bacon and garlic and set aside.

In the same skillet, let the butter melt and mix-in the flour. Gradually add the cream and milk and whisk until the sauce thickens. Add the cheese.

Reduce the heat to a simmer and keep the mixture simmering while you prepare the rest of the ingredients.

When you are ready to serve, add the drained pasta, bacon bits, roasted red peppers to the sauce. Stir to coat. Add pasta evenly to each serving plate. Top with some chicken and shrimp. Garnish with fresh parsley. Serve with fresh shredded Romano or Parmesan cheese.

Nutrition:
- 488 calories
- 6.7g carbs
- 33g proteins

8. Chicken Marsala

Preparation Time: 10 minutes
Cooking Time: 40 minutes
Servings: 4 - 6

Ingredients
· 2 tablespoons olive oil
· 2 tablespoons butter
· 4 boneless skinless chicken breasts
· 1 ½ cups sliced mushrooms
· 1 small clove garlic, thinly sliced
· Flour for dredging
· Sea salt and freshly ground black pepper
· 1 ½ cups chicken stock
· 1 ½ cups Marsala wine
· 1 tablespoon lemon juice
· 1 teaspoon Dijon mustard

Directions
Chicken scaloppini
Pound out the chicken with a mallet or rolling pin to about ½ inch thick. In a large skillet, heat the olive oil and 1 tablespoon of the butter over medium-high heat. When the oil is hot, dredge the chicken in flour. Season with salt and pepper on both sides. Dredge only as many as will fit in the skillet. Don't overcrowd the pan.

Cook chicken in batches, about 1 to 2 minutes on each side or until cooked through. Remove from skillet, and place on an oven-proof platter. Keep warm in the oven, while the remaining chicken is cooking.

Marsala sauce
In the same skillet, add 1 tablespoon of olive oil. On medium-high heat, sauté mushrooms and garlic until softened. Remove the mushrooms from the pan and set aside.

Add the chicken stock and loosen any remaining bits in the pan. On high heat, let reduce by half, about 6-8 minutes. Add Marsala wine and lemon juice and in the same manner reduce by half, about 6–8 minutes. Add the mushroom back in the saucepan, and stir in the Dijon mustard. Warm for 1 minute on medium-low heat. Remove from heat, stir in the remaining butter to make the sauce silkier.

To serve, pour the sauce over chicken, and serve immediately.

Nutrition:
- 487 calories
- 7.1g carbs
- 34g protein

9. Chicken Scampi

Preparation Time: 10 minutes
Cooking Time: 20 minutes
Servings: 4

Ingredients
Pasta
- ½ pound uncooked angel hair pasta
- ½ teaspoon canola or olive oil
- ¼ teaspoon salt

Chicken
- 1-pound chicken tenderloins
- ½ cup all-purpose flour
- ¼ teaspoon salt
- ⅛ teaspoon ground pepper
- ¼ teaspoon Italian seasoning
- ⅓ cup whole milk
- 2 tablespoons oil
- Vegetables and sauce
- 2 tablespoons canola or olive oil
- ½ green pepper, sliced into thin strips
- ½ red pepper, sliced into thin strips
- ½ yellow pepper, sliced into thin strips
- ½ red onion, sliced thin
- 5 tablespoons unsalted butter
- 6 cloves garlic, minced
- ¾ cup wine
- 1⅓ cups chicken broth
- ⅔ cup half and half
- ¼ teaspoon ground pepper
- 1 teaspoon salt
- ¼ teaspoon Italian seasoning

Directions

Cook the angel hair pasta according to package instructions. Drain and set aside.

To make the chicken, mix the flour, salt, pepper, and Italian seasoning in a bowl. Place the milk in a separate bowl. Lightly pound the chicken tenders, then coat them in flour. Dip into milk and dredge in flour once more.

In a large skillet, heat the oil over high heat. Cook each side of the chicken for about 2 minutes. Remove from heat and keep warm.

To make the vegetables and sauce, heat the oil in the skillet. Add the peppers and red onion. Sauté for 2 minutes over medium-high heat, stirring occasionally. Add the butter and minced garlic to the vegetables. Sauté for 1 more minute. Add the wine and broth. Reduce heat to medium-low. Let cook for 5 minutes. Add half and half, salt, pepper, and Italian seasoning. Let cook for 1 minute. Add the chicken and pasta. Toss together to blend well. Simmer to warm, then serve.

Nutrition:
- 489 calories
- 6.8g carbs
- 31g protein

10. Chicken Margherita

Preparation Time: 35 minutes
Cooking Time: 25 minutes
Servings: 6

Ingredients
Chicken
- 6 (4-ounce) boneless chicken breasts
- 2 cups water
- ¼ cup salt
- ¼ cup sugar

Pesto
- 2 cups fresh basil
- 1 clove garlic
- 2 tablespoons pecorino romano cheese, grated
- 3–4 tablespoons extra-virgin olive oil
- 1 tablespoon pine nuts (optional)
- Lemon garlic sauce
- 2 tablespoons butter
- 2 cloves garlic, minced
- 1 tablespoon all-purpose flour
- 1 tablespoon lemon juice
- ½ cup low-sodium chicken broth
- Chicken Margherita assembly
- 6 (4-ounce) grilled boneless chicken breasts
- ½ cup prepared pesto
- 1 cup grape tomatoes, halved
- 6 ounces fresh mozzarella, sliced
- ½ cup prepared lemon garlic sauce
- Freshly shredded parmesan cheese, for garnish

Directions

In a Ziploc bag, combine the water, salt, and sugar. Mix well. Add the chicken and refrigerate for at least 2 hours.

Grill chicken until cooked thoroughly. Set aside. Blend all pesto ingredients in a food processor to achieve a smooth consistency. Add 1 tablespoon of oil, if needed. Refrigerate in a sealed container until ready to use.

To make the lemon garlic sauce, melt the butter in a small saucepan. Add garlic and sauté for 1 minute. Slowly add some flour and stir well. Add fresh lemon juice and chicken broth. Stir for about 3–5 minutes until the sauce begins to thicken. Keep refrigerated.

To assemble the Chicken Margherita, preheat oven to 425°F. Move the grilled chicken to a baking dish and top with mozzarella cheese, pesto, and halved grape tomatoes.

Pour the lemon garlic sauce on top. Bake until cheese melts, about 10–15 minutes. To serve, sprinkle with freshly grated parmesan cheese, if desired.

Nutrition:
- 469 calories
- 6.3g carbs
- 31g protein

11. Chicken Carbonara

Preparation Time: 20 minutes
Cooking Time: 30 minutes
Servings: 4

Ingredients
- Marinated chicken or shrimp
- 1 cup extra-virgin olive oil
- 1 cup hot water
- 1 tablespoon Italian seasoning
- 1 tablespoon chopped garlic
- 3 pounds chicken strips or large shrimp, peeled and deveined

Sauce
- 1 cup butter
- 1½ teaspoons garlic, chopped
- 3 tablespoons bacon bits
- 3 tablespoons all-purpose flour
- 1 cup parmesan cheese, grated
- 1-quart heavy cream
- 1-quart milk
- ¼ cup bacon base
- ½ teaspoon black pepper
- 1¾ pounds long pasta (spaghetti, linguine, etc.) cooked according to package **Directions**
- ¼ teaspoon salt

Topping
- 3 tablespoons romano cheese, grated
- 3 tablespoons parmesan cheese, grated
- 1¾ cups mozzarella cheese, shredded
- ½ cup panko breadcrumbs
- 1½ teaspoons garlic, chopped
- 1½ tablespoons butter, melted
- 2 tablespoons parsley, chopped
- Marinated chicken strips (or shrimp) as above
- 1½ cups roasted red peppers, cut into small

strips
- ¼ cup bacon bits

Directions

Preheat oven to 350°F. In a mixing bowl, whisk together olive oil with hot water, Italian seasoning, and chopped garlic. Let chicken/shrimp marinate for at least 30 minutes in the refrigerator.

To make the sauce, melt the butter over medium heat in a large saucepan. Sauté the garlic and bacon bits for 5 minutes, stirring frequently.

Add the flour, parmesan cheese, heavy cream, milk, bacon base, pepper, and salt. Whisk well. Bring to a boil, then reduce heat and allow to simmer.

To make the topping, mix the romano cheese, parmesan, mozzarella cheese, panko, chopped garlic, melted butter, and chopped parsley in a mixing bowl. Blend well. Set aside.

Heat a large skillet to cook the chicken and/or shrimp. Add the red peppers and bacon bits. Cook for 3 minutes or until meat is cooked through. Add sauce and stir.

Add pasta. Mix well to coat the pasta evenly. Top with extra cheese, if desired. Serve.

Nutrition:

- 510 calories
- 6.3g carbs
- 30g protein

12. Turkey 'N Stuffing

Preparation Time: 20 minutes
Cooking Time: 1 hour 10 minutes
Servings: 4

Ingredients

- 4 cups day-old cornbread
- 2 cups day-old biscuits
- ⅓ cup chopped onion
- 1 cup diced celery
- 2 tablespoons dried parsley flakes
- 1 teaspoon poultry seasoning
- 1 teaspoon ground sage
- ½ teaspoon coarse ground pepper
- ¼ cup butter or margarine, melted
- 24 ounces chicken broth
- Cooking spray for greasing
- 8 cooked thick turkey breast slices
- 1 cup cranberry sauce
- Favorite sides such as green beans and mashed potatoes
- Gravy
- 3 tablespoons butter
- ½ cup diced onions
- 2 tablespoons all-purpose flour
- ¼ teaspoon salt
- ¼ teaspoon pepper
- ⅛ teaspoon dry sage flakes
- ⅛ teaspoon dry parsley flakes
- 1¼ cups milk

Directions

Preheat oven to 400°F and spray an 8x8-inch baking dish with cooking spray. In a food processor, add the cornbread and the biscuits. Process until you get a coarse consistency. Alternatively, grate the cornbread and biscuits with a large hole hand grater.

In a large bowl, stir together the onion, celery, grated cornbread and biscuits, parsley, poultry seasoning, sage, and pepper. Add the butter and chicken broth to the dry stuffing and mix to combine well.

Spread the stuffing evenly to the prepared baking dish. Bake uncovered for 1 hour or until golden brown. Warm-up the turkey in foil in the oven for 15-20 minutes or until warmed through.

Prepare the gravy by whisking the dry gravy ingredients together in a bowl. Melt the butter in a saucepan over medium heat and add the onions. Stir fry over medium-low heat until fragrant and tender. Add the dry ingredients. Whisk continuously, stirring thoroughly to remove lumps. When the flour begins to brown, slowly whisk in the milk. Continue cooking and whisking for about 2-3 minutes or until the mixture thickens.

To serve, add two slices of turkey to each plate and top with some gravy. Add some stuffing, top with some more of the gravy. Add some cranberry sauce and favorite sides.

Nutrition:
- 328 calories
- 16g carbs
- 34g protein

CHAPTER 8
Old and Modern
Bread Recipes

1. Ranchero Chicken Tacos

Preparation Time: 15 minutes
Cooking Time: 15 minutes
Servings: 8

Ingredients
- Cheddar cheese, shredded
- Flour tortillas
- Chicken breast, sliced

For Ranchero Sauce
- 2 garlic cloves, chopped
- 1 Serrano or jalapeno chili, seeded & diced
- ¼ cup of chopped onion
- 3 cups tomatoes, diced
- ½ teaspoon ground chili
- 1 tablespoon oregano
- 2 tablespoons cooking oil

Directions
For Ranchero Sauce:
Over moderate heat in a large saucepan; heat the oil until hot & then sauté the onions, garlic, and Serrano for a couple of minutes.
Decrease the heat & add in the tomatoes; stir well & cook until the tomatoes have wilted for 5 to 6 minutes. Add the seasonings & let simmer for 5 minutes more.
For Quesadilla
Sauté or grill the chicken. Mix the chicken with the prepared sauce. Butter the outside of your tortilla. Add the chicken-ranchero sauce filling and cheese. Fold the tortilla & cook in a hot skillet. Serve hot & enjoy.

Nutrition:
- 869 calories
- 58g total fats
- 38g protein

2. Beef Bacon Ranch Quesadillas

Preparation Time: 25 minutes
Cooking Time: 35 minutes
Servings: 4

Ingredients
- 1 package cooked bacon, finely chopped
- Ranch dressing bottled
- 1 package Mexican cheese or cheddar, shredded
- 4 chicken breasts (baked or grilled), finely chopped
- 1-2 packages whole-grain or tortillas flour

Directions
While you are baking or grilling the chicken until completely cooked, brown the bacon in a large skillet until turn golden brown and cooked through; set aside at room temperature to cool.

Finely chop the chicken and bacon. Using low-fat cooking spray, lightly coat your heated griddle & place two tortillas down to brown. Lightly drizzle the ranch over the tortillas.

Sprinkle the chicken and bacon onto the ranch, top with the shredded cheese. Place a tortilla on top, smooch down with your hand to set it together, & carefully flip. Once both sides are browned, remove them from the heat and transfer them onto a large plate.

Once done, cut each one up into triangle sections using a super-sharp knife or pizza cutter, roughly eight triangles per tortilla.

Nutrition:
- 879 calories
- 55g total fats
- 38g protein

3. Chicken Enchiladas

Preparation Time: 10 minutes
Cooking Time: 30 minutes
Servings: 6

Ingredients
- 3 chicken breasts cooked & cubed
- 1 cup masa harina corn tortilla mix
- 2 cans chicken broth (14.5 oz each)
- 1 cup mild red enchilada sauce
- 1-2 teaspoon garlic, minced
- ½ teaspoon chili powder
- 1 teaspoon onion powder
- 16 oz Velveeta cheese, cubed
- ½ teaspoon cumin
- 3 cup water, divided
- 1 teaspoon salt

For Garnish:
- Corn tortilla strips & tomatoes

Directions
Sauté the garlic in a large pot for a couple of minutes. Add in the chicken broth. Whisk the masa harina with 2 cups water in a medium bowl until blended well. Add the masa mixture into the pot.

Add the cubed Velveeta cheese, enchilada sauce, leftover water, onion powder, cumin, chili powder & salt. Bring the mixture to a boil. Add the cubed chicken; decrease the heat & let simmer for half an hour. Garnish with tortilla strips and tomatoes; serve immediately & enjoy.

Nutrition:
- 888 calories
- 61g total fats
- 39g protein

4. Chicken Fajitas

Preparation Time: 15 minutes
Cooking Time: 30 minutes
Servings: 6

Ingredients
For Vegetable Finishing Sauce:
- 2 tablespoon water
- ½ teaspoon lime juice, fresh
- 5 boneless skinless chicken breasts
- 2 large white onions sliced into ½" strips
- 3 bell peppers sliced into ½" strips
- Flour tortillas
- 2 teaspoon soy sauce
- ¼ teaspoon black pepper
- 2 tablespoon olive oil
- ¼ teaspoon salt

For Chicken Marinade:
- ⅓ cup lime juice, freshly squeezed
- 1 teaspoon garlic, minced
- ½ teaspoon liquid smoke
- 1 tablespoon white vinegar
- ½ teaspoon chili powder
- 1 tablespoon soy sauce
- ½ teaspoon cayenne pepper
- 2 tablespoon vegetable oil
- ¼ teaspoon onion powder
- 1 teaspoon salt
- ⅓ cup water
- ¼ teaspoon black pepper

For Toppings, Optional:
- Grated cheddar cheese, salsa, guacamole, sour cream, Pico de Gallo, shredded lettuce

Directions

Combine the entire Chicken Marinade ingredients together in a small bowl; whisk well until completely combined. Pierce each chicken breast in several places using a large fork & then place the chicken breasts in a glass baking dish, medium-sized. Add the Chicken Marinade to the baking dish; cover & let it refrigerate overnight.

Over medium-high heat in a large cast iron skillet; heat the olive oil until hot & sauté the peppers for 5 to 7 minutes, then add the onions. Continue to sauté until onions & peppers turn soft, for 15 to 20 minutes more, stirring every now and then.

In the meantime, place a separate fry pan or skillet over medium-high heat. Place the marinated chicken breasts into the hot pan & cook for 15 to 20 minutes, until done, flipping after every 10 minutes.

Whisk the entire Vegetable Finishing Sauce **ingredients** together in a small bowl. When the onions and peppers are done; decrease the heat to medium-low and add in the Vegetable Finishing Sauce; let simmer for a couple of more minutes.

Once chicken breasts are cooked through, transfer them to a clean, large cutting board & slice it thinly. Place the onions, peppers, and chicken on a flour tortilla. Top with the optional topping ingredients, as desired. Serve immediately & enjoy.

Nutrition:

- 891 calories
- 62.3g total fats
- 41.3g protein

5. Mushroom Jack Chicken Fajitas

Preparation Time: 10 minutes
Cooking Time: 45 minutes
Servings: 4

Ingredients
For Chipotle Garlic Butter:
- 8 garlic cloves, finely minced
- ¼ cup canned chipotle peppers
- 1 teaspoon each of ground black pepper & salt
- ⅓ cup unsalted butter, softened

For Caramelized Onions:
- 1 ½ tablespoons white sugar
- 6 medium yellow or white onions; sliced into ¼ to ½" thick slices; separating them into rings
- 1 ½ tablespoons balsamic vinegar
- ¼ cup vegetable stock
- 1 ½ tablespoons butter, unsalted
- ½ teaspoon salt
- 1 ½ tablespoons vegetable oil

For Fajitas:
- 2 pounds chicken breast, boneless and skinless
- 1 tablespoon chipotle powder
- 2 tablespoons Cajun seasoning
- 1 teaspoon ground black pepper
- 2 cups green peppers
- ⅓ cup fresh cilantro, minced
- 2 tablespoons vegetable oil
- 1 cup Monterey Jack cheese, shredded
- 2 cups cremini mushrooms, sliced
- ½ cup green onion, minced
- Ground black pepper & salt to taste
- 2 tablespoons lime juice, freshly squeezed
- 1 ½ teaspoons salt

To Serve:
- ½ cup sour cream

- 12 corn or flour tortillas
- ¼ cup canned jalapeños, sliced
- 1 cup Monterey Jack cheese, shredded
- ¼ cup guacamole

Directions

Caramelize the Onions:

Over moderate heat in a shallow pan; heat the butter until melted. Scatter the sliced onions on top of the melted butter and then drizzle with the oil; slowly cook for 8 to 10 minutes, until turn translucent.

Decrease the heat to medium-low; give the onions a good stir and add the vinegar and sugar; toss & stir until mixed well.

After 10 minutes of cooking, pour in the broth. To prevent the onions from burning, don't forget to scrape up any caramelized bits from the bottom of your pan & stir every now and then.

Once the onions are browned well & very soft, after 10 to 15 minutes more of cooking, remove them from the heat.

Preparing the Butter:

Now, over medium heat in a small saucepan, heat 2 tablespoons of the butter until melted and then add the minced garlic; cook for 8 to 10 minutes, until the garlic turns fragrant and begins to brown.

Remove the butter from heat and place in the fridge until chilled, for 15 minutes. In a small bowl, combine the garlic butter together with softened butter, chipotle & salt.

Mash all the **ingredients** together using a large fork. Season the mixture with more salt & ground black pepper, if required. Using a plastic wrap, cover the seasoned butter & store it in the fridge until ready to use.

For the Fajitas:

Slice the chicken breast into ½" strips, rubbing them

with the chipotle powder, Cajun seasoning, lime juice, pepper, and salt. Let rest while you heat the pan.

Now, over high heat in a cast iron pan; heat half of the oil until it starts to shimmer, add half of the chicken strips; cook until cooked through & well-browned. Transfer the cooked chicken to a plate & cook the leftover chicken strips.

Add the sliced mushrooms to the hot pan; ensure that you don't add more of oil or rinse the mushrooms. Bring the heat to medium-high & cook until the mushrooms turn brown & begin to crisp, undisturbed. Sprinkle them with a very small quantity of salt.

Carefully flip the mushrooms & continue to cook for 5 to 7 more minutes, until both sides turn browned & they are completely cooked. Transfer them to the plate with the cooked chicken.

Add the leftover oil to the hot pan. When it starts to shimmer and starts to smoke, add in the green peppers & lightly sprinkle them with a very small amount of salt, stirring occasionally.

When the peppers begin to soften, push them so that they sit around the edge of the pan; decrease the heat to low.

Add the caramelized onions to the middle of your pan, pushing them so that the peppers and onions cover any exposed portions of the pan.

Place the cooked chicken strips over the onions. Dot the onions, peppers, and chicken with the chipotle butter sauce.

Sprinkle the chicken with the shredded cheese. Layer the cooked mushrooms on top of the cheese & dot the mushrooms with ½ to 1 tablespoon more of butter.

Cover the pan with a lid & let it sit for 5 minutes on low heat. Once the chicken is warmed through & the cheese is completely melted, scatter the cilantro and green onions on top.

Serve the fajitas immediately in the cast iron pan.

Warm the tortillas & serve the salsa, jalapeños, sour cream, guacamole, and extra cheese on the side.

Nutrition:
- 894 calories
- 60.9g total fats
- 40.9g protein

6. *Game Day Chili*

Preparation Time: 25 minutes
Cooking Time: 3 hours and 5 minutes
Servings: 13

Ingredients
- 1 can tomato paste (6-ounce)
- 2 pounds ground chuck
- 1 onion, medium, chopped
- 3 cans tomato sauce (8-ounce)
- 1 can beef broth (14 ½ ounce)
- 2 cans pinto beans, rinsed & drained (15-ounce)
- 1 can chopped green chilis (4.5-ounce)
- 3 - 4 garlic cloves, minced
- 1 bottle dark beer (12-ounce)
- 2 tablespoons chili powder
- 1 tablespoon Worcestershire sauce
- 2 teaspoons ground cumin
- 1 teaspoon paprika
- 1 to 2 teaspoons ground red pepper
- Pickled jalapeño pepper slices, for garnish
- 1 teaspoon hot sauce

Directions
Cook ground chuck together with chopped onion and minced garlic cloves over medium heat in a Dutch oven, stirring frequently until the meat crumbles & is no longer pink from inside; drain well.

Combine the meat mixture with beans & the leftover **ingredients** (except the one for garnish) in the Dutch oven; bring everything together to a boil. Decrease the heat & let simmer until thickened for 3 hours. Garnish the recipe with pickled jalapeno pepper slices.

Nutrition:
- 884 calories
- 58g total fats
- 40g protein

7. Cinnamon Crunch Scone

Preparation Time: 25 minutes
Cooking Time: 10 minutes
Servings: 12

Ingredients
- 2 ½ teaspoons baking powder
- ⅓ cup sugar
- 3 ¼ cups all-purpose flour
- 1 ½ sticks cold butter, cubed (¾ cup)
- 1 cup buttermilk
- 2 tablespoon butter, melted
- ½ teaspoon baking soda
- 2 cups or DIY cinnamon chips or 1 package cinnamon baking chips (10 ounces)
- ½ teaspoon salt

For the Glaze:
- 5 cup powdered sugar
- ½ cup milk
- 1 tablespoon cinnamon
- 1 teaspoon vanilla extract
- pinch of salt

For Cinnamon Chips:
- 2 tablespoon vegetable shortening
- ⅔ cup sugar
- 3 tablespoon cinnamon
- 2 tablespoon light corn syrup

Directions
Preheat your oven to 425 F in advance.
Combine flour together with sugar, baking soda, baking powder, and salt in a large bowl; mix well. Cut in the butter & blend into the flour mixture using a pastry cutter or a fork until the mixture looks like coarse crumbs. Stir in the buttermilk; mix with the remaining ingredients until everything is just moist.

Fold in the cinnamon chips and make sure that they are distributed evenly.

Turn to a slightly floured surface & start kneading the dough for 10 to 12 minutes, until the dough is no longer crumbly. Roll the dough into a long rectangle, and the dough is approximately ½" thick & cut into triangles. Place on well sprayed or well-greased baking sheets and then brush the tops with butter. Bake in the preheated oven for 12 to 15 minutes. Once done, place them on a cooling rack and let them cool before dipping into the glaze.

For the Glaze: Mix the powdered sugar together with vanilla extract, cinnamon, milk & a pinch of salt until a smooth glaze form. Take the cooled scones and dip into the glaze and place them on the baking sheet again. Repeat these steps until you have successfully covered the scones.

For the Chips: Combine sugar together with corn syrup, shortening, and cinnamon in a bowl; give everything a good stir until combined well. Preheat your oven to 200 F. Spread the mixture onto a well-greased parchment paper lined baking sheet into a rectangle that is approximately ¼" thick. Bake until the mixture is hot and melted together for 35 minutes. Let completely cool and then cut into desired pieces using a sharp knife or pizza well. Store in an airtight container until ready to serve.

Nutrition:
- 851 calories
- 58g total fats
- 39g protein

CHAPTER 9
Side Salad Recipes

1. Caribbean Shrimp Salad

Preparation Time: 20 minutes
Cooking Time: 55 minutes
Servings: 4

Ingredients:
- 8 cups baby spinach, fresh
- ¼ cup lime juice, freshly squeezed
- 2 tablespoons chili garlic sauce
- ½ teaspoon paprika
- 4 cups cooked shrimp
- 5 tablespoons seasoned rice vinegar, divided
- ½ teaspoon ground cumin
- 1 cup peeled mango, chopped
- ½ cup green onions, thinly sliced
- 2 garlic cloves, minced
- 1 cup radishes, julienne-cut
- ¼ cup peeled avocado, diced
- 2 tablespoons pumpkinseed kernels, unsalted 1 ½ tablespoons olive oil
- Dash of salt

Directions:
In a large bowl; combine the cooked shrimp together with chili garlic sauce
& 2 tablespoons of vinegar; toss well. Cover & let chill for an hour.
Now, in a small bowl, combine the leftover vinegar together with garlic cloves, oil, lime juice, lime rind, ground cumin, paprika & salt, stirring well with a whisk.
Place 2 cups of spinach on each of 4 plates; top each serving with a cup of the prepared shrimp mixture. Arrange ¼ cup radishes, ¼ cup mango & 1 tablespoon of the avocado around the shrimp on each plate. Top each serving with approximately 1 ½ teaspoons of

pumpkinseed kernels & 2 tablespoons of green onions. Drizzle each salad with approximately 2 tablespoons of the vinaigrette. Serve and enjoy.

Nutrition:
- 124 Calories
- 76.9g Fat
- 67.9g Carbs
- 45.8g Protein

2. Southwest Caesar Salad

Preparation Time: 10 minutes
Cooking Time: 20 minutes
Servings: 6

Ingredients:
- 2 tablespoons mayonnaise
- ¼ teaspoon cayenne or ground red pepper
- 6 cups fresh romaine lettuce, washed
- ⅓ cup parmesan cheese, grated
- 1 cup croutons
- ½ of a red bell pepper, cut into thin strips
- 1 cup whole kernel corn, frozen & thawed
- ½ cup fresh cilantro, chopped
- 2 tablespoons green onion, chopped
- ¼ cup olive oil
- 2 tablespoon lime juice, freshly squeezed
- 1/8 teaspoon salt

Directions:
Place onions together with mayo, ground red pepper, lime juice, and salt in a blender or food processor; cover & process until blended well. Slowly add the oil at the top using the feed tube & continue to process after each addition until blended well.
Toss the lettuce with the corn, croutons, bell peppers, cheese, and cilantro in a large bowl.
Add the mayo mixture; evenly toss until nicely coated.
Serve immediately & enjoy.

Nutrition:
- 265 Calories
- 62g Fat
- 98g Carbs
- 47g Protein

3. Red Beans from Popeye's

Preparation Time: 20 minutes
Cooking Time: 40 minutes
Servings: 10

Ingredients:
- 3 14-ounce cans red beans
- ¾ pounds smoked ham hock
- 1¼ cups water
- ½ teaspoon onion powder
- ½ teaspoon garlic salt
- ¼ teaspoon red pepper flakes
- ½ teaspoon salt
- 3 tablespoons lard
- Steamed long-grain rice

Directions:
Add 2 canned red beans, ham hock, and water to the pot. Cook on medium heat and let simmer for about 1 hour.

Remove from heat and wait until the meat is cool enough to handle. Then remove meat from the bone. In a food processor, add meat, cooked red beans and water mixture, onion powder, garlic salt, red pepper, salt, and lard. Pulse for 4 seconds. You want the beans to be cut, and the liquid thickened. Drain the remaining 1 can red beans and add to the food processor. Pulse for only 1 or 2 seconds.

Remove **ingredients** from the food processor and transfer to the pot from earlier.

Cook on low heat, stirring frequently until mixture is heated through. Serve over steamed rice.

Nutrition:
- 445 Calories
- 12g Fat
- 67g Carbs
- 9g Fibers

4. Café Rio's Sweet Pork Barbacoa Salad

Preparation Time: 10 minutes
Cooking Time: 8 minutes
Servings: 8

Ingredients:
- 3 pounds pork loin
- Garlic salt, to taste
- 1 can root beer
- ¼ cup water
- ¾ cup brown sugar
- 1 10-ounce can red enchilada sauce
- 1 4-ounce can green chilies
- ½ teaspoon chili powder
- 8 large burrito size tortillas
- 1½ serving Cilantro Lime Rice
- 1 can black beans, drained and heated
- 2 heads Romaine lettuce, shredded
- 1½ cups tortilla strips
- 1 cup Queso Fresco cheese
- 2 limes, cut in wedges
- ¼ cup cilantro

Dressing:
- ½ packet Hidden Valley Ranch Dressing Mix 1 cup mayonnaise
- ½ cup milk
- ½ cup cilantro leaves
- ¼ cup salsa Verde
- ½ jalapeno pepper, deseeded
- 1 plump clove garlic
- 2 tablespoons fresh lime juice

Directions:

Sprinkle garlic salt on pork. Put in the slow cooker with the flat side facing down.

Add ¼ cup root beer and water. Cover and cook on low setting for 6 hours.

To prepare sauce, add the rest of the root beer, brown sugar, enchilada sauce, green chilies, and chili powder in a blender. Blend until smooth.

Remove meat from slow cooker then transfer onto the cutting board. Shred, discarding juices and fat.

Return shredded pork to slow cooker with the sauce. Cook on low setting for another 2 hours. When there is only about 15 to 20

minutes left to cook, remove the lid to thicken the sauce.

To prepare the dressing, mix all dressing **ingredients** in a blender. Puree until smooth. Then, transfer to the refrigerator and allow to chill for at least 1 hour.

To assemble the salad, layer tortilla, rice, beans, pork, lettuce, tortilla strips, cheese, and dressing in a bowl. Serve with a lime wedge and cilantro leaves.

Nutrition:

- 756 Calories
- 28g Fat
- 91g Carbs
- 7g Fibers

5. Almond Crusted Salmon Salad

Preparation Time: 15 minutes
Cooking Time: 30 minutes
Servings: 4

Ingredients:
- ¼ cup olive oil
- 4 (4 -ounce) portions salmon
- ½ teaspoon kosher salt
- ⅛ teaspoon ground black pepper
- 2 tablespoons garlic aioli (bottled is fine)
- ½ cup chopped and ground almonds for crust
- 10 ounces kale, chopped
- ¼ cup lemon dressing of choice
- 2 avocados, peeled, pitted, and cut into ½-inch pieces 2 cups cooked quinoa
- 1 cup brussels sprouts, sliced
- 2 ounces arugula
- ½ cup dried cranberries
- 1 cup balsamic vinaigrette
- 24 thin radish slices
- Lemon zest

Directions:
In a large skillet, heat the olive oil over medium-high heat. Sprinkle the salmon with salt and pepper to season. When the skillet is hot, add the fish fillets and cook for about 3 minutes on each side or until it flakes easily with a fork. Top the salmon with garlic aioli and sprinkle with nuts.

Meanwhile, combine all the salad ingredients, including the quinoa, in a bowl, and toss with the dressing.

Serve the salad with a fish fillet on top of greens and sprinkle with radishes and lemon zest.

Nutrition:
- 243 Calories
- 45g Fat
- 23g Carbs
- 52g Protein

6. Deep Fried Pickles from Texas Roadhouse

Preparation Time: 10 minutes
Cooking Time: 10 minutes
Servings: 4

Ingredients
- Vegetable oil, for deep frying
- ¼ cup flour
- 1¼ teaspoons Cajun seasoning, divided
- ¼ teaspoon oregano
- ¼ teaspoon basil
- ⅛ teaspoon cayenne pepper
- Kosher salt
- 2 cups dill pickles, drained and sliced
- ¼ cup mayonnaise
- 1 tablespoon horseradish
- 1 tablespoon ketchup

Directions:
Preheat about 1½ inches oil to 375°F in a large pot.

In a separate bowl, make the coating by combining flour, 1 teaspoon Cajun seasoning, oregano, basil, cayenne pepper, and Kosher salt.

Dredge pickle slices in flour mixture. Lightly shake to remove any excess, then carefully lower into the hot oil. Work in batches so as not to overcrowd the pot. Deep fry for about 2 minutes or until lightly brown.

Using a slotted spoon, transfer pickles to a plate lined with paper towels to drain.

While pickles drain and cool, add mayonnaise, horseradish, ketchup, and remaining Cajun seasoning in a bowl. Mix well. Serve immediately with dip on the side.

Nutrition:
- 296 Calories
- 28g Total fat
- 12g Carbs
- 1g Protein

7 Chicken Teriyaki Salad

Preparation Time: 5 minutes
Cooking Time: 5 minutes
Servings: 4-5

Ingredients:
- 2 boneless, skinless chicken breasts
- ½ cup store-bought teriyaki marinade

For assembly
- 8 slices of cucumber
- 1/4 cup Black olives
- 1/4 cup Banana Peppers, sliced
- ¼ cup Green Pepper sliced thinly
- ½ red onion thinly sliced
- 1 whole Tomato, thinly sliced or grape tomatoes

1/3 cup
- 300g lettuce
- 200 g baby spinach
- Sweet Onion Sauce
- 1 tablespoon red wine vinegar
- 1/3 cup light corn syrup
- 1 tablespoon white vinegar
- 2 tablespoon minced white onion
- 2 teaspoon balsamic vinegar
- ½ tsp garlic powder
- 1/4 teaspoon salt
- 4 teaspoon brown sugar
- ½ teaspoon lemon juice
- 1/8 tsp black pepper
- 1/4 teaspoon poppy seeds

Directions:

Put teriyaki marinade and chicken breast in a bowl and marinate for at least 30 minutes. While the chicken is marinating, prepare the sweet onion sauce by combining everything in a pan and heat them until it boils. Cool down. Slice all vegetables for the salad and set aside. Grill or panfry chicken and brush with marinade once in a while. Once cooked, slice into strips or cubes. Mix and toss everything in a bowl and serve immediately.

Nutrition:
- 240 Calories
- 3g Fat
- 4g Fiber
- 35g Carbs
- 20g Protein

CHAPTER 10
Old and Modern
Sweet and Savory
Snack Recipes

1. Papa John's Cinnapie

Preparation Time: 5 minutes
Cooking Time: 12 minutes
Servings: 12

Ingredients
- 1 whole pizza dough
- 1 tablespoon melted butter
- 2 tablespoons cinnamon, or to taste

Topping
- ¾ cup flour
- ½ cup white sugar
- 1/3 cup brown sugar
- 2 tablespoons oil
- 2 tablespoons shortening

Icing
- 1½ cups powdered sugar
- 3 tablespoons milk
- ¾ teaspoon vanilla

Directions:
Preheat oven to 460°F. Grease or spray a pizza pan or baking sheet.
Brush the dough evenly with melted butter. Sprinkle with cinnamon. Place the **ingredients** for the topping in a bowl and toss together with a fork.
Sprinkle topping over the dough. Bake until fragrant and lightly browned at the edges (about 10–12 minutes). Mix the icing **ingredients** together in a bowl. If too thick, gradually add in a little more milk. Drizzle icing over warm pizza.

Nutrition:
- 560 Calories
- 90g Carbs
- 19g Fat
- 8g Protein

2. Olive Garden's Cheese Ziti Al Forno

Preparation Time: 10 minutes
Cooking Time: 35 minutes
Servings: 8

Ingredients:
- 1 lb. Ziti
- 4 tbsp Butter
- 2 cloves Garlic
- 4 tbsp All-purpose flour
- 2 cups Half & Half
- A dash of Black pepper
- Kosher salt (as desired)
- 3 cups Marinara
- 1 cup - grated Parmesan - divided
- 2 cups Shredded mozzarella - divided

Other Shredded Cheese:
- ½ cup Fontina
- ½ cup Romano
- ½ cup Ricotta
- ½ cup Panko breadcrumbs

The garnish:
- Fresh Parsley

Directions:
Warm the oven to reach 375° Fahrenheit.
Spritz the casserole dish with cooking oil spray. Prepare a large pot of boiling - salted water to cook the ziti until al dente. Drain and set it to the side.
Mince the garlic. Shred/grate the cheese and chop the parsley.
Make the alfredo. Heat the skillet using the medium temperature setting to melt the butter. Toss in the garlic to sauté for about half a minute. Whisk in flour and simmer until the sauce is bubbling (1-2 min.).
Whisk in the Half-and-Half and simmer. Stir in ½ cup

parmesan, pepper, and salt. Cook it until the sauce thickens (2-3 min.). Stir in the marinara, one cup of mozzarella, Romano, fontina, and ricotta. Fold in the pasta. Dump it into the casserole dish.

Combine ½ cup of the parmesan and the breadcrumbs. Sprinkle it over the top of the dish. Set the timer and bake until browned as desired and bubbly (30 min.). Garnish with parsley and serve.

Nutrition:
- 272 Calories
- 20g Fat
- 25g Carbs
- 23g Protein

3. Chipotle's Refried Beans

Preparation Time: 5 minutes
Cooking Time: 5 minutes
Servings: 6

Ingredients
- 1-pound dried pinto beans
- 6 cups warm water
- ½ cup bacon fat
- 2 teaspoons salt
- 1 teaspoon cumin
- ½ teaspoon black pepper
- ½ teaspoon cayenne pepper

Directions
Rinse and drain the pinto beans. Check them over and remove any stones. Place the beans in a Dutch oven and add the water. Bring the pot to a boil, reduce the heat, and simmer for 2 hours, stirring frequently.
When the beans are tender, reserve ½ cup of the boiling water and drain the rest. Heat the bacon fat in a large, deep skillet. Add the beans 1 cup at a time, mashing and stirring as you go. Add the spices and some of the cooking liquid if the beans are too dry.

Nutrition:
- 100 Calories
- 18g Carbs
- 1g Fat
- 6g Protein

4. Low Fat Veggie Quesadilla

Preparation Time: 10 minutes
Cooking Time: 5 minutes
Servings: 2

Ingredients
- ½ tablespoon canola oil
- ½ cup mushrooms, chopped
- ½ cup carrot, grated
- 1/3 cup broccoli, sliced
- 2 tablespoons onion, finely chopped
- 1 tablespoon red bell pepper, finely chopped
- 1 teaspoon soy sauce
- 1 dash cayenne pepper
- 1 dash black pepper
- 1 dash salt
- 2 flour tortillas
- ¼ cup cheddar cheese, grated
- ¼ cup mozzarella cheese, grated
- ¼ cup sour cream
- ¼ cup salsa, medium or mild to taste
- ¼ cup shredded lettuce

Directions:
Heat oil in a large skillet. Add mushrooms, carrots, broccoli, onion, and bell pepper. Stir-fry over medium-high heat for about 5 minutes. Pour in soy sauce, then season with cayenne, salt, and pepper. Transfer vegetables onto a plate. Set aside.

In the same skillet, heat first tortilla. Top with cheddar and mozzarella cheeses, followed by the cooked vegetables. Cover with the second tortilla. Cook for about 1 minute on each side or until cheeses are runny. Cut into slices. Serve hot with sour cream, salsa, and shredded lettuce on the side.

Nutrition:
- 186 Calories
- 12g Fat
- 18g Carbs
- 25g Protein

5. Garlic Mashed Potatoes

Preparation Time: 20 minutes
Cooking Time: 1 hour
Servings: 4

Ingredients

- 1 medium-sized bulb garlic, fresh
- 2 pounds red-skinned potatoes
- ½ cup milk
- ½ cup heavy cream
- ¼ cup butter
- Salt and pepper to taste

Directions:

Preheat the oven to 400°F. Wrap whole garlic bulb with aluminum foil and bake it for 45 minutes, until the garlic softens. Remove it from the oven and let it cool in its wrapping.

Once cool, unwrap the garlic, peel off the outer layer, and squeeze the cooked pulp out. Set it aside. In the meantime, cut the potatoes and wash them, don't remove the skin and put them in a saucepan. Add water just to cover the potatoes. Boil until it cooks thoroughly for about 20 minutes.

Drain the water and add the other **ingredients**. Use the hands to mash. Lumps can be left, depending on your preference. Serve.

Nutrition:

- 254 Calories
- 16g Fat
- 24g Carbs
- 31g Protein

6. Vegetable Medley

Preparation Time: 15 minutes
Cooking Time: 10 minutes
Servings: 4

Ingredients

- ½ pound cold, fresh zucchini, sliced in half-moons
- ½ pound cold, fresh yellow squash, sliced in half-moons
- ¼ pound cold red pepper, julienned in strips ¼-inch thick
- ¼ pound cold carrots, cut into ¼-inch strips a few inches long
- ¼ pound cold red onions, thinly sliced
- 1 cold, small corn cob, cut crosswise in 1" segments
- 3 tablespoons cold butter or margarine
- 1 teaspoon salt
- 1 teaspoon sugar
- ½ teaspoon granulated garlic
- 1 teaspoon Worcestershire sauce
- 1 teaspoon soy sauce
- 2 teaspoons fresh or dried parsley

Directions:

Wash, peel, and cut your vegetables as appropriate. In a saucepan, heat the butter over medium-high heat. Once it is hot, add salt, sugar, and garlic. Add the carrots, squash, and zucchini, and when they start to soften, add the rest of the vegetables and cook for a couple of minutes.

Add the Worcestershire sauce, soy sauce, and parsley. Stir to combine and coat the vegetables. When all the vegetables are cooked to your preference, serve.

Nutrition:
- 276 Calories
- 21g Fat
- 22g Carbs
- 30g Protein

7. Big Ol' Brownie

Preparation Time: 10 minutes
Cooking Time: 1 hour 10 minutes
Servings: 4

Ingredients
- 1 can of brownie mix
- Ice cream, vanilla, to serve
- Hot Caramel sauce, to serve

Directions:
Set the oven's temperature to exactly 350° F; cut the foil strips to line the giant muffin tin cups;
Lay the strips in crisscross-layer form for use as a handle for lifting when the brownies are made. Spray the foil in the kitchen spray pan; Prepare the brownie batter as indicated. Divide the batter between the muffin pans. The muffin cups can be about ¾ full;
Set the muffin pan on a heating sheet with the edges and start baking in the preheated oven for 40 to 50 minutes approximately; Remove the muffin pan from your oven and let it cool in the mold for 5 minutes approximately, then take to a rack to cool for another 10 minutes;
To loosen the sides of each brownie, you can use an icing spatula or a knife and then use the handles to lift the muffin pan. Serve a hot brownie on a plate with hot caramel sauce and a scoop of vanilla ice cream.

Nutrition:
- 206 Calories
- 24g Fat
- 24g Carbs
- 29g Protein

8. Mozzarella Cheese Sticks Recipe

Preparation Time: 5 minutes
Cooking Time: 5 minutes
Servings: 10

Ingredients
- ¼ cup flour
- 1 cup breadcrumbs
- 2 eggs
- 1 tablespoon milk
- 500 g mozzarella cheese
- 1 cup of vegetable oil
- 1 cup marinara sauce

Directions:
Gather all the elements of mozzarella cheese sticks then mix eggs and milk together in a medium bowl.
Cut the mozzarella into sticks 2 x 2 cm thick.
Cover each mozzarella cane with flour. Then dip them inside the egg and then within the breadcrumbs.
Dip the mozzarella sticks lower back into the egg and skip them in breadcrumbs.
Take to the freezer earlier than frying. Heat the oil within the pan and prepare dinner the mozzarella cheese sticks for approximately a minute on every aspect or until well browned.
Drain the cheese sticks on paper napkins and serve with marinara sauce or pizza sauce.

Nutrition:
- 168 calories
- 19g total fats
- 12g protein

CHAPTER 11
Old and Modern
Fruit Salad Recipes

1. Fruit Salad with Lemon Foam

Preparation Time: 30 minutes
Cooking Time: 0 minutes
Servings: 4

Ingredients:
- 4th ripe nectarines
- 200 g Raspberries
- 1 tbsp Pistachio nuts
- 4th very fresh egg yolk (size M)
- 4 tbsp sugar
- Juice of 1 lemon
- 1/8 l prosecco (or non-alcoholic sparkling wine)

Directions:
Peel the nectarines with a small sharp knife and cut the pulp into slices from the stone. Read out the raspberries, wash them carefully, and drain them on kitchen paper. Spread the fruit mixed in four glasses or on dessert plates. Roughly chop the pistachios.
Prepare a saucepan with a suitable metal mixing bowl for a hot water bath, pour approx. 5 cm of water into the saucepan and heat. Mix the egg yolks in the bowl with the sugar and whisk for 3-4 minutes with the whisk of the hand mixer.
Place the bowl over the hot water bath and pour the lemon juice and prosecco into the egg yolk cream while stirring continuously until an airy foam form. Pull out the bowl from the water bath and continue to beat the foam for 1-2 minutes until it is only lukewarm. Pour the lemon foam over the fruit salads and sprinkle the pistachios. Serve the dessert immediately.

Nutrition:
- 225 calories
- 17.1g fats
- 4g protein

2. Vegan Amaranth Pudding with Fruit Salad

Preparation Time: 60 minutes
Cooking Time: 0 minutes
Servings: 4

Ingredients:
- 200 g Amaranth grains
- 1 l soy milk
- 6 Apricots
- 2 tbsp Walnut kernels
- 4 tbsp Pomegranate seeds
- 60 g sugar
- Cinnamon powder
- 3 tbsp food starch
- 2 pack Bourbon vanilla sugar
- 1 pinch salt
- 300 g cold soy cream
- 1 pack Cream fixer

Directions:
For the pudding on the evening before, cover the amaranth with sufficient water and let it swell for 12 hours. Pour into a colander the next day and drain. Boil the amaranth and soy milk in a saucepan, then cover and simmer over low heat for 25 minutes.

In the meantime, wash, halve, stone and cut the apricots for the fruit salad and cut them into wedges. Roughly chop the walnut kernels. Mix the apricot slices, nuts, pomegranate seeds, and 1 tablespoon of sugar, season with a pinch of cinnamon.

Mix the starch, vanilla sugar, remaining sugar, salt, and ½ tsp cinnamon. Stir the mix into the amaranth and let simmer for about 2 minutes. Let the pudding mixture cool lukewarm in the pot.

Whisk the soy cream with the hand mixer until foamy. Sprinkle in the cream fixer and continue beating until the cream is firm and foamy. Fold the whipped cream under the pudding mixture. Fill the pudding in four glasses and arrange the fruit salad on it.

Nutrition:
- 248 calories
- 14g fats
- 6g protein

3. Quick Fruit Salad with Sabayon

Preparation Time: 30 minutes
Cooking Time: 0 minutes
Servings: 4

Ingredients:
- 2nd fully ripe figs
- 1 kiwi
- 100 g each seedless blue and green grape
- 100 g Strawberries
- 1 pear
- 6 tbsp freshly squeezed lime juice
- 2nd Egg yolks
- 1 tbsp sugar
- grated peel of 1 organic lime
- 1 tbsp chopped almonds

Directions:
Wash the figs and quarter them lengthways. Peel the kiwi, quarter lengthways and slice transversely. Wash the grapes, pluck from the stems and cut in half.
Briefly rinse, clean, and halve the strawberries. Quarter the pear, core, peel, and cut into fine slices. Arrange the fruit decoratively on four plates, drizzle with 2 tablespoons of lime juice.
Mix the egg yolks with the sugar, 2 tablespoons of warm water, and the remaining lime juice and the grated lime peel in the kettle and beat in a hot, non-boiling water bath until the mixture is thick and creamy.
Remove from the water bath, continue to beat for 1-2 minutes next to the stove and spread lukewarm over the fruit. Sprinkle with the almonds.

Nutrition:
- 135 calories
- 14g fats
- 5g protein

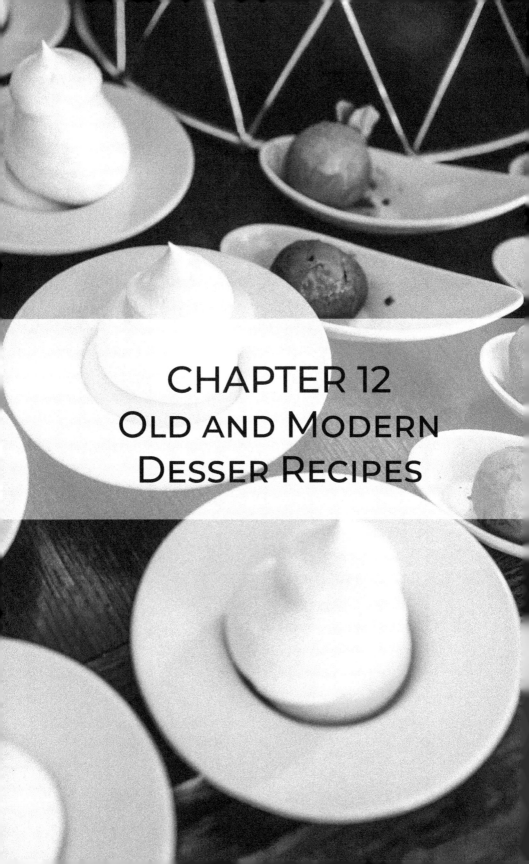

CHAPTER 12
Old and Modern Desser Recipes

1. *Chocolate Mousse Dessert Shooter*

Preparation Time: 30 minutes
Cooking Time: 0 minutes
Servings: 4

Ingredients
- 2 tablespoons butter
- 6 ounces semi-sweet chocolate chips (1 cup), divided
- 2 eggs
- 1 teaspoon vanilla
- 8 Oreo® cookies
- ½ cup prepared fudge sauce
- 2 tablespoons sugar
- ½ cup heavy cream
- Canned whipped cream

Directions
Melt the butter and all but 1 tablespoon of the chocolate chips in a double boiler.
When they are melted, stir in the vanilla and remove from the heat.
Whisk in the egg yolks.
Beat the egg whites until they form soft peaks, and then fold them into the chocolate mixture.
Beat the sugar and heavy cream in a separate bowl until it forms stiff peaks or is the consistency that you desire. Fold this into the chocolate mixture.
Crush the remaining chocolate chips into small pieces and stir them into the chocolate. Crush the Oreos. (You can either scrape out the cream from the cookies or just crush the entire cookie.)
Spoon the cookie crumbs into the bottom of your cup and pat them down. Layer the chocolate mixture on top. Finish with whipped cream and either more chocolate chips or Oreo mixture.

Store in the refrigerator until ready to serve.

Nutrition:
- 41g carbs
- 12g fats
- 2g protein

2. Cinnamon Apple Turnover

Preparation Time: 10 minutes
Cooking Time 25 minutes
Servings: 4-6

Ingredients
- 1 large Granny Smith apple, peeled, cored, and diced
- ½ teaspoon cornstarch
- ¼ teaspoon cinnamon
- Dash ground nutmeg
- ¼ cup brown sugar
- ¼ cup applesauce
- ¼ teaspoon vanilla extract
- 1 tablespoon butter, melted
- 1 sheet of puff pastry, thawed
- Whipped cream or vanilla ice cream, to serve

Directions
Preheat the oven to 400°F. Prepare a baking sheet by spraying it with non-stick cooking spray or using a bit of oil on a paper towel.

In a mixing bowl, mix together the apples, cornstarch, cinnamon, nutmeg, and brown sugar. Stir to make sure the apples are well covered with the spices. Then stir in the applesauce and the vanilla.

Lay out your puff pastry and cut it into squares. You should be able to make 4 or 6 depending on how big you want your turnovers to be and how big your pastry is.

Place some of the apple mixture in the center of each square and fold the corners of the pastry up to make a pocket. Pinch the edges together to seal. Then brush a bit of the melted butter over the top to give the turnovers that nice brown color.

Place the filled pastry onto the prepared baking

pan and transfer to the preheated oven. Bake 20–25 minutes, or until they become a golden brown in color. Serve with whipped cream or vanilla ice cream.

Nutrition:
- 42g carbs
- 13g fats
- 4g protein

3. Cherry Chocolate Cobbler

Preparation Time: 10 minutes
Cooking Time: 45 minutes
Servings: 8

Ingredients
- 1½ cups all-purpose flour
- ½ cup sugar
- 2 teaspoons baking powder
- ½ teaspoon salt
- ¼ cup butter
- 6 ounces semisweet chocolate morsels
- ¼ cup milk
- 1 egg, beaten
- 21 ounces cherry pie filling
- ½ cup finely chopped nuts

Directions
Preheat the oven to 350°F. Combine the flour, sugar, baking powder, salt, and butter in a large mixing bowl. Use a pastry blender to cut the mixture until there are lumps the size of small peas.
Melt the chocolate morsels. Let cool for approximately 5 minutes, then add the milk and egg and mix well. Beat into the flour mixture, mixing completely. Spread the pie filling in a 2-quart casserole dish. Randomly drop the chocolate batter over the filling, then sprinkle with nuts.
Bake for 40–45 minutes. Serve with a scoop of vanilla ice cream if desired.

Nutrition:
- 45g carbs
- 14g fats
- 3g protein

4. Pumpkin Custard with Gingersnaps

Preparation Time: 30 minutes
Cooking Time 35 minutes
Servings: 8

Ingredients
- Custard
- 8 egg yolks
- 1¾ cups (1 15-ounce can) pure pumpkin puree
- 1¾ cups heavy whipping cream
- ½ cup sugar
- 1½ teaspoons pumpkin pie spice
- 1 teaspoon vanilla

Topping
- 1 cup crushed gingersnap cookies
- 1 tablespoon melted butter

Whipped Cream
- 1 cup heavy whipping cream
- 1 tablespoon superfine sugar (or regular sugar if you have no caster sugar)
- ½ teaspoon pumpkin pie spice

Garnish
- 8 whole gingersnap cookies

Directions
Preheat the oven to 350°F. Separate the yolks from 8 eggs and whisk them together in a large mixing bowl until they are well blended and creamy.

Add the pumpkin, sugar, vanilla, heavy cream, and pumpkin pie spice and whisk to combine. Cook the custard mixture in a double boiler, stirring until it has thickened enough that it coats a spoon.

Pour the mixture into individual custard cups or an 8×8-inch baking pan and bake for about 20 minutes if using individual cups or 30–35 minutes for the baking pan, until it is set and a knife inserted comes out clean.

While the custard is baking, make the topping by combining the crushed gingersnaps and melted butter. After the custard has been in the oven for 15 minutes, sprinkle the gingersnap mixture over the top.

When the custard has passed the clean knife test, remove from the oven, and let cool to room temperature. Whisk the heavy cream and pumpkin pie spice together with the caster sugar and beat just until it thickens. Serve the custard with the whipped cream and garnish each serving with a gingersnap.

Nutrition:
- 44g carbs
- 14g fats
- 3g protein

5. Baked Apple Dumplings

Preparation Time: 20 minutes
Cooking Time 40 minutes
Servings: 2–4

Ingredients
- 1 (17½ ounce) package frozen puff pastry, thawed
- 1 cup sugar
- 6 tablespoons dry breadcrumbs
- 2 teaspoons ground cinnamon
- 1 pinch ground nutmeg
- 1 egg, beaten
- 4 Granny Smith apples, peeled, cored, and halved
- Vanilla ice cream for serving

Icing
- 1 cup confectioners' sugar
- 1 teaspoon vanilla extract
- 3 tablespoons milk

Pecan Streusel
- ⅔ cup chopped toasted pecans
- ⅔ cup packed brown sugar
- ⅔ cup all-purpose flour
- 5 tablespoons melted butter

Directions
Preheat the oven to 425°F. When the puff pastry has completely thawed, roll out each sheet to measure 12 inches by 12 inches. Cut the sheets into quarters. Combine the sugar, breadcrumbs, cinnamon, and nutmeg together in a small bowl.

Brush one of the pastry squares with some of the beaten egg. Add about 1 tablespoon of the breadcrumb mixture on top, then add half an apple, core side down, over the crumbs. Add another tablespoon of the breadcrumb mixture.

Seal the dumpling by pulling up the corners and pinching the pastry together until the seams are totally sealed. Repeat this process with the remaining squares. Assemble the **ingredients** for the pecan streusel in a small bowl.

Grease a baking sheet or line it with parchment paper. Place the dumplings on the sheet and brush them with a bit more of the beaten egg. Top with the pecan streusel.

Bake for 15 minutes, then reduce heat to 350°F and bake for 25 minutes more or until lightly browned. Make the icing by combining the confectioners' sugar, vanilla, and milk until you reach the proper consistency.

When the dumplings are done, let them cool to room temperature and drizzle them with icing before serving.

Nutrition:
- 43g carbs
- 13g fats
- 3.1g protein

6. *Peach Cobbler*

Preparation Time: 10 minutes
Cooking Time 45 minutes
Servings: 4

Ingredients
- 1¼ cups Bisquick
- 1 cup milk
- ½ cup melted butter
- ¼ teaspoon nutmeg
- ½ teaspoon cinnamon
- Vanilla ice cream, for serving

Filling
- 1 (30-ounce) can peaches in syrup, drained
- ¼ cup sugar

Topping
- ½ cup brown sugar
- ¼ cup almond slices
- ½ teaspoon cinnamon
- 1 tablespoon melted butter

Directions
Preheat the oven to 375°F. Grease the bottom and sides of an 8×8-inch pan. Whisk together the Bisquick, milk, butter, nutmeg, and cinnamon in a large mixing bowl. When thoroughly combined, pour into the greased baking pan.

Mix together the peaches and sugar in another mixing bowl. Put the filling on top of the batter in the pan. Bake for about 45 minutes.

In another bowl, mix together the brown sugar, almonds, cinnamon, and melted butter. After the cobbler has cooked for 45 minutes, cover evenly with the topping and bake for an additional 10 minutes. Serve with a scoop of vanilla ice cream.

Nutrition:
- 41g carbs
- 13g fats
- 4g protein

7. Campfire S'mores

Preparation Time: 15 minutes
Cooking Time: 40 minutes
Servings: 9

Ingredients
Graham Cracker Crust
- 2 cups graham cracker crumbs
- ¼ cup sugar
- ½ cup butter
- ½ teaspoon cinnamon
- 1 small package brownie mix (enough for an 8×8-inch pan)

Brownie Mix
- ½ cup flour
- ⅓ cup cocoa
- ¼ teaspoon baking powder
- ¼ teaspoon salt
- ½ cup butter
- 1 cup sugar
- 1 teaspoon vanilla
- 2 large eggs

S'mores Topping
- 9 large marshmallows
- 5 Hershey candy bars
- 4½ cups vanilla ice cream
- ½ cup chocolate sauce

Directions
Preheat the oven to 350°F.

Mix together the graham cracker crumbs, sugar, cinnamon, and melted butter in a medium bowl. Stir until the crumbs and sugar have combined with the butter.

Line an 8×8-inch baking dish with parchment paper. Make sure to use enough so that you'll be able to lift the baked brownies out of the dish easily. Press the graham cracker mixture into the bottom of the lined pan.

Place the pan in the oven to prebake the crust a bit while you are making the brownie mixture.

Melt the butter over medium heat in a large saucepan, then stir in the sugar and vanilla. Whisk in the eggs one at a time. Then whisk in the dry ingredients, followed by the nuts. Mix until smooth. Take the crust out of the oven, pour the mixture into it, and bake for 23–25 minutes. When brownies are done, remove from oven and let cool in the pan.

After the brownies have cooled completely, lift them out of the pan using the edges of the parchment paper. Be careful not to crack or break the brownies. Cut into individual slices.

When you are ready to serve, place a marshmallow on top of each brownie and broil in the oven until the marshmallow starts to brown. You can also microwave for a couple of seconds, but you won't get the browning that you would in the broiler.

Remove from the oven and top each brownie with half of a Hershey bar. Serve with ice cream and a drizzle of chocolate sauce.

Nutrition:
- 41g carbs
- 12g fats
- 4g protein

8. Banana Pudding

Preparation Time: 15 minutes plus 1 hour 30 minutes chilling time
Cooking Time: 0 minutes
Servings: 8–10

Ingredients
- 6 cups milk
- 5 eggs, beaten
- ¼ teaspoon vanilla extract
- 1⅛ cups flour
- 1½ cups sugar
- ¾ pound vanilla wafers
- 3 bananas, peeled
- 8 ounces whipped cream

Directions
In a large saucepan, heat the milk to about 170°F.
Mix the eggs, vanilla, flour, and sugar together in a large bowl. Very slowly add the egg mixture to the warmed milk and cook until the mixture thickens to a custard consistency.
Layer the vanilla wafers to cover the bottom of a baking pan or glass baking dish. You can also use individual portion dessert dish or glasses.
Layer banana slices over the top of the vanilla wafers. Be as liberal with the bananas as you want.
Layer the custard mixture on top of the wafers and bananas. Move the pan to the refrigerator and cool for 1½ hours. When ready to serve, spread Cool Whip (or real whipped cream, if you prefer) over the top. Garnish with banana slices and wafers if desired.
Nutrition:
- 45g carbs
- 14g fats
- 3g protein

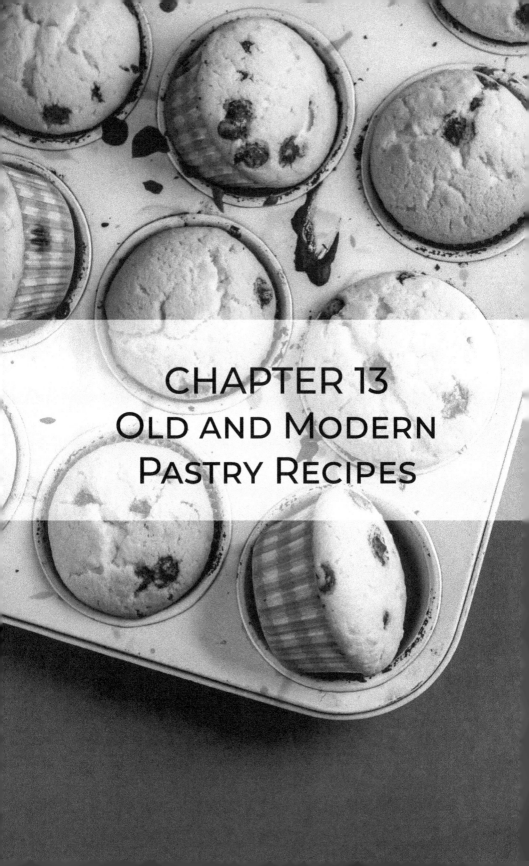

CHAPTER 13
Old and Modern Pastry Recipes

1. Carrot Cake Cheesecake

Preparation Time: 20 minutes plus 5 hours chilling time
Cooking Time: 50–60 minutes
Servings: 8

Ingredients
Cheesecake
- 2 (8-ounce) blocks cream cheese, at room temperature
- ¾ cup granulated sugar
- 1 tablespoon flour
- 3 eggs
- 1 teaspoon vanilla

Carrot Cake
- ¾ cup vegetable oil
- 1 cup granulated sugar
- 2 eggs
- 1 teaspoon vanilla
- 1 cup flour
- 1 teaspoon baking soda
- 1 teaspoon cinnamon
- 1 dash salt
- 1 (8-ounce) can crushed pineapple, well-drained with juice reserved
- 1 cup grated carrot
- ½ cup flaked coconut
- ½ cup chopped walnuts

Pineapple Cream Cheese Frosting
- 2 ounces cream cheese, softened
- 1 tablespoon butter, softened
- 1 ¾ cups powdered sugar
- ½ teaspoon vanilla
- 1 tablespoon reserved pineapple juice

Directions

Preheat the oven to 350°F and grease a 9-inch springform pan. In a large bowl, beat together the cream cheese and the sugar until smooth. Then beat in the flour, eggs, and vanilla until well combined. Set aside.

In another large bowl, beat together the ¾ cup vegetable oil, sugar, eggs, and vanilla until smooth. Then add the flour, baking soda, cinnamon, and salt and beat until smooth. Fold in the crushed pineapple, grated carrot, coconut, and walnuts.

Pour 1 ½ cups of the carrot cake batter into the prepared pan. Drop a large spoonful of the cream cheese batter over the top of the carrot cake batter. Then add a spoonful of carrot cake batter over the top of the cream cheese batter. Repeat with the remaining batter.

Bake the cake for 50–60 minutes, or until the center is set. Remove it from the oven and cool for about an hour before taking out the sides of the springform pan. Refrigerate for at least 5 hours.

While the cake is cooling, make the frosting. Beating together all the frosting **ingredients**. Frost the cake when it is completely cold.

Nutrition:

- 40g carbs
- 11g fats
- 6g protein

2. Original Cheesecake

Preparation Time: 4 hours 15 minutes
Cooking Time: 1 hour 5 minutes
Servings: 12

Ingredients
Crust:
- 1 ½ cups graham cracker crumbs
- ¼ teaspoon ground cinnamon
- ⅓ cup margarine, melted

Filling:
- 4 (8-ounce) packages cream cheese, softened
- 1 ¼ cups white sugar
- ½ cup sour cream
- 2 teaspoons vanilla extract
- 5 large eggs

Topping:
- ½ cup sour cream
- 2 teaspoons sugar

Directions:
Preheat the oven to 475°F and place a skillet with half an inch of water inside. Combine the ingredients for the crust in a bowl. Line a large pie pan with parchment paper, and spread crust onto the pan. Press firmly. Cover it with foil, and keep it in the freezer until ready to use.

Combine all the ingredients for the filling EXCEPT the eggs in a bowl. Scrape the sides of the bowl while beating, until the mixture is smooth. Mix in eggs one at a time, and beat until fully blended.

Take the crust from the freezer and pour in the filling, spreading it evenly. Place the pie pan into the heated skillet in the oven, and bake for about 12 minutes.

Reduce the heat to 350°F. Continue to bake for about 50 minutes, or until the top of the cake is golden.

Remove it from the oven and transfer the skillet onto a wire rack to cool.

Prepare the topping by mixing all ingredients in a bowl. Coat the cake with the topping, then cover. Refrigerate for at least 4 hours. Serve cold.

Nutrition:
- 41g carbs
- 11g fats
- 2g protein

3. Ultimate Red Velvet Cheesecake

Preparation Time: 3 hours 30 minutes
Cooking Time: 1 hour 15 minutes
Servings: 16

Ingredients
Cheesecake:
- 2 (8-ounce) packages cream cheese, softened
- ⅔ cup granulated white sugar
- Pinch salt
- 2 large eggs
- ⅓ cup sour cream
- ⅓ cup heavy whipping cream
- 1 teaspoon vanilla extract
- Non-stick cooking spray
- Hot water, for water bath

Red velvet cake:
- 2 ½ cups all-purpose flour
- 1 ½ cups granulated white sugar
- 3 tablespoons unsweetened cocoa powder
- 1 ½ teaspoons baking soda
- 1 teaspoon salt
- 2 large eggs
- 1 ½ cups vegetable oil
- 1 cup buttermilk
- ¼ cup red food coloring
- 2 teaspoons vanilla extract
- 2 teaspoons white vinegar

Frosting:
- 2 ½ cups powdered sugar, sifted
- 2 (8-ounce) packages cream cheese, softened
- ½ cup unsalted butter, softened
- 1 tablespoon vanilla extract

Directions:

For the cheesecake, preheat the oven to 325°F. Beat the cream cheese, sugar, and salt for about 2 minutes, until creamy and smooth. Add the eggs, mixing again after adding each one. Add the sour cream, heavy cream, and vanilla extract, and beat until smooth and well blended.

Coat a springform pan with non-stick cooking spray, then place parchment paper on top. Wrap the outsides entirely with two layers of aluminum foil. (This is to prevent water from the water bath from entering the pan.)

Pour the cream cheese batter into the pan, then place it in a roasting pan. Add boiling water to the roasting pan to surround the springform pan. Place it in the oven and bake for 45 minutes until set.

Transfer the springform pan with the cheesecake onto a rack to cool for about 1 hour. Refrigerate overnight.

For the red velvet cake, preheat the oven to 350°F. Combine the flour, sugar, cocoa powder, baking soda, and salt in a large bowl. In a separate bowl, mix the eggs, oil, buttermilk, food coloring, vanilla, and vinegar. Add the wet **ingredients** to dry **ingredients**. Blend for 1 minute with a mixer on medium-low speed, then on high speed for 2 minutes.

Spray non-stick cooking spray in 2 metal baking pans that are the same size as the springform pan used for the cheesecake. Coat the bottoms thinly with flour. Divide the batter between them.

Bake for about 30–35 minutes. The cake is made when only a few crumbs are attached to a toothpick when inserted in the center. Transfer the cakes to a rack and let them cool for 10 minutes. Separate the cakes from the pans using a knife around the edges, then invert them onto the rack. Let them cool completely.

To prepare the frosting, mix the powdered sugar, cream cheese, butter, and vanilla using a mixer on medium-high speed, just until smooth.

Assemble the cake by positioning one red velvet cake layer onto a cake plate. Remove the cheesecake from the pan, peel off the parchment paper, and layer it on top of the red velvet cake layer. Top with the second red velvet cake layer.

Coat a thin layer of prepared frosting on the entire outside of the cake. Clean the spatula every time you scoop out from the bowl of frosting, so as to not mix crumbs into it. Refrigerate for 30 minutes to set. Then coat the cake with a second layer by adding a large scoop on top, then spreading it to the top side of the cake then around it. Cut into slices. Serve.

Nutrition:
- 39g carbs
- 12g fats
- 4g protein

4. *Strawberry Shortcake*

Preparation Time: 5 minutes
Cooking Time: 2 hours and 15 minutes
Servings: 16

Ingredients
Sugared Strawberries:
- 2 cups strawberries (sliced)
- ¼ cup granulated sugar

Whipped Cream:
- 4 cups heavy cream
- ½ cup powdered sugar
- ¼ teaspoon vanilla

Shortcake Biscuit:
- 4 ½ cups all-purpose flour
- ½ cup sugar
- 5 tablespoons baking powder
- 2 teaspoons salt
- 1 ¾ cups butter
- 2 cups heavy cream
- 2 cups buttermilk
- 2 scoops vanilla ice cream

Directions
Preheat the oven to 375°F. In a bowl, combine the sliced strawberries with the sugar. Stir, cover, and refrigerate for 2 hours. Chill a mixing bowl and beat the heavy cream, powdered sugar, and vanilla until soft peaks form. Don't over beat or you will lose the fluffy consistency. Refrigerate.

In a mixing bowl, mix together the flour, sugar, baking powder, and salt. Stir to combine. Using two butter knives, cut the butter into the flour mixture until it becomes crumbly. Add the cream and the buttermilk and mix gently until the batter forms.

Turn out the dough onto a floured surface, and roll it

to form biscuits about half an inch thick. Take care not to turn the cutter as you remove it from the dough. Place the biscuits on a non-stick cookie sheet and bake for about 15 minutes. They should at least double in size.

When they cool, assemble the shortcake by cutting each biscuit in half, topping the bottom half with strawberries and ice cream, and placing the top half of the biscuit on top of the ice cream. Top with more strawberries and whipped cream.

Nutrition:
- 40g carbs
- 12g fats
- 5g protein

5. Lemoncello Cream Torte

Preparation Time: 15 minutes
Cooking Time: 20 minutes plus 5 hours chilling time
Servings: 8 - 10

Ingredients
- 1 box yellow cake mix
- Limoncello liqueur (optional)
- 1 package ladyfinger cookies
- 1 (3-ounce) package sugar-free lemon gelatin
- 1 cup boiling water
- 1 (8-ounce) package cream cheese, softened
- 1 teaspoon vanilla extract
- 1 (13-ounce) can cold milnot (evaporated milk), whipped

For the glaze:
- 1 cup confectioner's sugar
- 1–2 tablespoons lemon juice

Directions
Preheat the oven to 350°F. Prepare the yellow cake mix according to the Directions on the package. Use two 9-inch round cake pans, or you can use a springform pan and cut the cake in half after it is baked.

When the cake is made and cooled, you can soak the layers lightly with some limoncello. Do the same with the ladyfingers. Bring one cup of water to a boil and stir in the lemon gelatin. Refrigerate until it gets thick, but don't let it set.

Mix together the cream cheese and vanilla, then mix in the thickened gelatin. Fold the whipped milnot into the mixture until combined. To assemble the cake, place the bottom layer of the cake back in the pan. This will help you get even layers. Top the cake with about half an inch of the lemon filling. Place ladyfingers on top of the filling, then top with another layer of the filling. Place the other half of the cake on the top.

Place the cake in the refrigerator to set. Make a drizzle with some lemon juice and confectioner's sugar, and drizzle over the cake.

Nutrition:
- 45g carbs
- 16g fats
- 5g protein

6. *Oreo Cookie Cheesecake*

Preparation Time: 10 minutes plus 4–6 hours chilling time
Cooking Time: 60 minutes
Servings: 8 - 10

Ingredients
- 1 package Oreo cookies
- ⅓ cup unsalted butter, melted
- 3 (8-ounce) packages cream cheese
- ¾ cup granulated sugar
- 4 eggs
- 1 cup sour cream
- 1 teaspoon vanilla extract
- Whipped cream and additional cookies for garnish

Directions
Preheat the oven to 350°F. Crush most of the cookies (25-30) in a food processor or blender, and add the melted butter. Press the cookie mixture into the bottom of a 9-inch springform pan and keep it in the refrigerator while you prepare the filling.

In a mixing bowl, beat the cream cheese until smooth, and add the sugar. Beat in the eggs in one a time. When the eggs are mixed together, beat in the sour cream and vanilla.

Chop the remaining cookies and fold them gently into the filling mixture. Pour the filling into the springform pan and bake at 350°F for 50–60 minutes. Ensure the center of the cake has set.

Let the cake cool for 15 minutes, then carefully remove the sides of the springform pan. Transfer to the refrigerator and refrigerate for 4–6 hours or overnight.

Nutrition:
- 47g carbs
- 18g fats
- 8g protein

7. Blackout Cake

Preparation Time: 30 minutes
Cooking Time: 35–45 minutes
Servings: 8 - 10

Ingredients

For the Cake:

- 1 cup butter, softened
- 4 cups sugar
- 4 large eggs
- 4 teaspoons vanilla extract, divided
- 6 ounces unsweetened chocolate, melted
- 4 cups flour
- 4 teaspoons baking soda
- ½ teaspoon salt
- 1 cup buttermilk
- 1 ¾ cups boiling water

For the Chocolate Ganache:

- 12 ounces semisweet chocolate, chips or chopped
- 3 cups heavy cream
- 4 tablespoons butter, chopped
- 2 teaspoons vanilla
- 1 ½ cups roasted almonds, crushed (for garnish)

Directions

Preheat the oven to 350°F. Prepare two large rimmed baking sheets with parchment paper (or grease and dust with flour 3 8-inch cake pans).

In a large bowl or bowl for a stand mixer, beat together the butter and sugar until well combined. When the sugar mixture is fluffy, add the eggs and 2 teaspoons of vanilla. When that is combined, add the 4 ounces of melted chocolate and mix well.

In a separate bowl, stir together the flour, baking soda, and salt. Gradually add half the flour mixture to the chocolate mixture. When it is combined, add half of the buttermilk and mix until combined. Repeat with remaining flour mixture and buttermilk. When it is completely combined, add the boiling water and mix thoroughly. (The batter should be a little thin).

Divide the batter evenly between the two large baking sheets that you prepared earlier (or 3 8-inch cake pans).

Transfer to the oven and bake for 20–30 minutes for the baking sheets or 25-35 minutes for the cake pans, or until a toothpick inserted in the center comes out clean.

Remove from the oven and let cakes cool for about 10 minutes. With the pastry ring, make 3 cakes from each of the baking sheets. When they are completely cool down. If using cake pans, turn them out onto a cooling rack and let them cool completely and then cut horizontally into two to make 6 cake layers.

Make the ganache by mixing the chocolate chips and cream in a heat-safe glass bowl. Place the bowl over a pot of boiling water. Reduce heat to medium-low and let simmer gently. Stir constantly with a wooden spoon until the chocolate is all melted. Add-in the butter and vanilla and stir until well combined. Let cool for a few minutes, cover with plastic wrap, and refrigerate until the ganache holds its shape and is spreadable, about 10 minutes.

To assemble the cake, place the first cake layer on a serving plate and spread some of the ganache on the top. Place the second cake layer on top and spread some of the ganache on top. Repeat until all 6 layers are done. Use the remaining ganache to frost the top and sides of the cake, then cover the sides with crushed almonds (if desired) by pressing them gently into the chocolate ganache. Refrigerate before serving.

Nutrition:

- 41g carbs
- 10g fats
- 4g protein

8. Molten Lava Cake

Preparation Time: 20 minutes
Cooking Time: 10 minutes
Servings: 5-6

Ingredients:
For the Cakes:
- Six tablespoons unsalted butter (2 tablespoons melted, four tablespoons at room temperature)
- 1/2 cup natural cocoa powder (not Dutch process), plus more for dusting
- 1 1/3 cups all-purpose flour
- One teaspoon baking soda
- 1/2 teaspoon baking powder
- 1/2 teaspoon salt
- Three tablespoons milk
- 1/4 cup vegetable oil
- 1 1/3 cups sugar
- 1 1/2 teaspoons vanilla extract
- Two large eggs, at room temperature

For the Fillings and Toppings:
- 8 ounces bittersweet chocolate, finely chopped
- 1/2 cup heavy cream
- Four tablespoons unsalted butter
- One tablespoon light corn syrup
- Caramel sauce, for drizzling
- 1-pint vanilla ice cream

Directions:
Oven preheats to 350 degrees F. Make the cakes: Brush four one 1/4-cup brioche molds (jumbo muffin cups or 10-ounce ramekins) with the butter melted in 2 tablespoons. Clean the cocoa powdered molds and tap the excess.

In a small bowl, whisk in the flour, baking soda, baking powder, and salt. Bring 3/4 cup water& the milk and over medium heat to a boil in a saucepan; set aside.

Use a stand mixer, combine vegetable oil, four tablespoons of room-temperature butter and sugar and beat with the paddle attachment until it's fluffy at medium-high speed, around 4 minutes, scrape the bowl down and beat as desired. Add 1/2 cup cocoa powder and vanilla; beat over medium velocity for 1 minute. Scrape the pot beneath. Add one egg and beat at medium-low speed for 1 minute, then add the remaining egg and beat for another minute.

Gradually beat in the flour mixture with the mixer on a low level, then the hot milk mixture. Finish combining the batter with a spatula of rubber before mixed. Divide the dough equally between the molds, each filling slightly more than three-quarters of the way.

Move the molds to a baking sheet and bake for 25 to 30 minutes, until the tops of the cakes feel domed, and the centers are just barely set. Move the baking sheet to a rack; allow the cakes to cool for about 30 minutes before they pull away from the molds.

How to set up the Cake: Make the Filling: Microwave the sugar, butter, chocolate, and corn syrup in a microwave-safe bowl at intervals of 30 seconds, stirring each time, until the chocolate starts to melt, 1 minute, 30 seconds. Let sit for three minutes and then whisk until smooth. Reheat, if possible, before use.

Using a paring knife tip to remove the cakes gently from the molds, then invert the cakes onto a cutting board.

Hollow out a spoon to the cake; save the scraps. Wrap the plastic wrap and microwave cakes until steaming, for 1 minute.

Drizzle the caramel plates, unwrap the cakes, then put them on top. Pour three tablespoons into each cake filling.

Plug in a cake scrap to the door. Save any leftover scraps or discard them.

Top each cake, use an ice cream scoop. Spoon more chocolate sauce on top, spread thinly so that it is coated in a jar.

Nutrition:
- 546 Calories
- 5g Protein
- 61g Carbohydrate
- 31g Fat

CHAPTER 14
Soft Drink Recipes

1. Rainforest Café's Strawberry Lemonade

Preparation Time: 5 minutes
Cooking Time: 5 minutes
Servings: 8

Ingredients:
- ¾ cup of sugar
- 1-pound strawberries, fresh, diced
- 6 cups water, chilled
- 1 lemon, zested
- 6 lemons, juiced

Directions:
Take a small saucepan, place it over medium-high heat, and then add berries in it. Pour in 1 cup water, stir in lemon zest and then bring the mixture to a boil. Transfer strawberry mixture into a pitcher, add remaining water along with lemon juice and then stir until combined. Taste to adjust sweetener if needed and then let it chill for 1 hour in the refrigerator before serving.

Nutrition:
- 487 Calories
- 132 g Carbohydrates
- 5 g Fiber
- 122 g Sugars

2. Chick-fil-A's Frozen Lemonade Copycat

Preparation Time: 10 minutes
Cooking Time: 0 minutes
Servings: 3

Ingredients
- 1/2 c. freshly squeezed lemon juice
- 1/2 c. sugar
- 2 c. water
- 6 c. vanilla ice cream
- sliced lemons, for garnish

Directions:
Dissolve the sugar in lemon juice. Add water and chill to dilute.
Stir lemonade and ice cream into a blender. Mix until smooth, and split between 3 cups. Garnish with lemon slices, and serve.

Nutrition:
- 470 calories
- 3g fiber
- 120g sugar

3. Mike's Hard Lemonade Copycat

Preparation Time: 15 minutes
Cooking Time: 0 minutes
Servings: 8

Ingredients
- 2-1/4 cups sugar
- 5 cups water, divided
- 1 tablespoon grated lemon zest
- 1-3/4 cups lemon juice
- 1 cup light rum or vodka
- 6 to 8 cups ice cubes

Garnish:
- Lemon slices

Directions:
Combine the sugar, 1 cup of water, and lemon zest into a large saucepan. Cook over medium heat and stir until sugar dissolves, about 4 minutes. Out of heat strip. Stir in the juice of the lemon and the remaining vapor. Offer in a 2-qt. Pitcher; leave to cool until chilled. Stir the rum in. Place 3/4 to 1 cup of ice in a highball glass for each serving. Pour lemonade into the glass. Garnish as desired, with lemon slices.

Nutrition:
- 402 calories
- 4.9g fiber
- 104.3g sugar

CONCLUSION

We have reached the end! We hope you enjoyed our cookbook and it gave you beautiful emotions. The most important advantage of using copycat restaurant recipes is that you can save money, but you can customize recipes if necessary. For example, if you want to reduce the salt or butter in one of the dishes, you can do it. People think you need a background in cooking or a degree in culinary arts to be able to cook those secret dishes. What better way to control the consistency of what you and your family shove into your mouth than by preparing your meals? Another advantage is that you will be able to cook together with your family members, which makes the family more united and peaceful. We hope you'll choose Sara Panera again to bring flavor to your meals.

Bye and see you next cookbook!

CPSIA information can be obtained
at www.ICGtesting.com
Printed in the USA
BVHW091413030521
606339BV00005B/660